ITALY OF MY DREAMS

MCMXCVIII

MATTHEW WHITE

ITALY OF MY DREAMS

*The Story of an American Designer's
Real-life Passion for Italian Style*

Photographs by Art Gray

PUBLISHER / EDITORIAL DIRECTOR: SUZANNE SLESIN
DESIGN: STAFFORD CLIFF
MANAGING EDITOR: JANE K. CREECH
PRODUCTION: DOMINICK J. SANTISE JR.
COPY EDITOR: ELIZABETH GALL

POINTED LEAF PRESS, LLC.

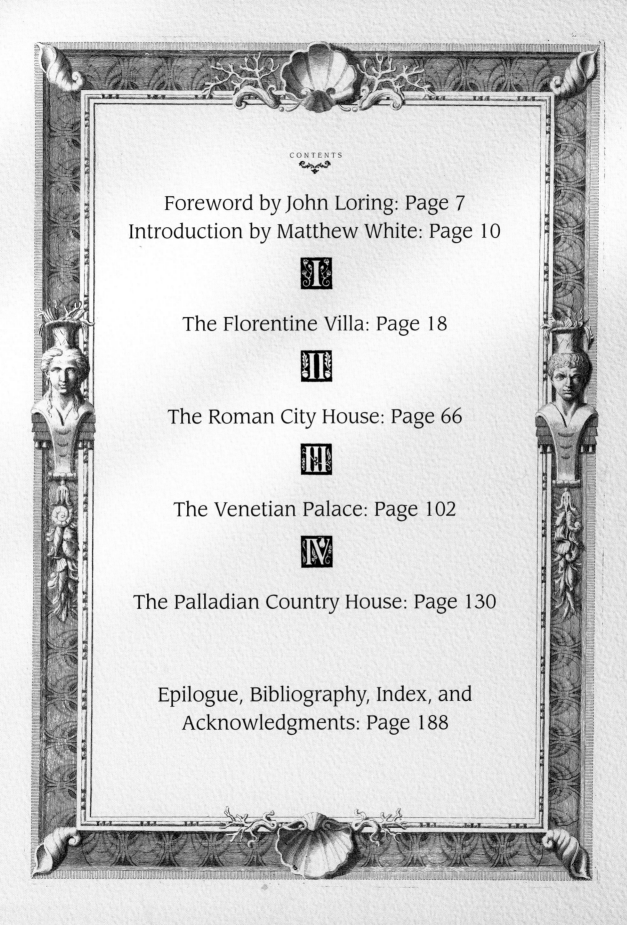

CONTENTS

Foreword by John Loring: Page 7
Introduction by Matthew White: Page 10

I

The Florentine Villa: Page 18

II

The Roman City House: Page 66

III

The Venetian Palace: Page 102

IV

The Palladian Country House: Page 130

Epilogue, Bibliography, Index, and
Acknowledgments: Page 188

OREWORD

AN AMERICAN LIFE INSPIRED BY ITALY

By John Loring

John Loring served as design director of Tiffany & Co. from 1979 to 2009. He has written twenty-two books on lifestyle and design and has been a contributing writer for Architectural Digest *for thirty-six years.*

"The American air ... favors sharp effects, disengages differences, preserves lights, defines ..." observed Henry James in his comments of 1905 in *The American Scene.* He was specifically commenting on, as he termed it, "the great Palladian pile" that America's champion of Italian Renaissance Revival style, the architect Stanford White, had just completed for Tiffany & Co. on Fifth Avenue and 37th Street in New York, where it still stands today. Inspired by Michele Sanmicheli's Palazzo Grimani in Venice, James praised its Italianate "high clearness," its "great nobleness," and its "sociable symmetry."

The Italian Renaissance Revival style finds a great champion today in New York designer Matthew White. His work holds "high clearness," "nobleness," and sociability in its own solid embrace while creating country villas and city apartments with the symmetry, proportion, order, continuity, and definition of the Italian Renaissance, all gracefully and poetically translated for the comforts of contemporary high-style living.

Matthew's introduction to Italy came on a third visit to Europe. The first trip was to Russia and Eastern Europe; the second, to France. The impressionable young American aesthete then found Italy "all I hoped it would be and more. It resonated with me on a very deep level. I thought Russian palaces were okay, but they're not Italy," he said. And there, as he progressed from Rome, with its somewhat daunting grandeur, to Florence, with its stately nobility, and on to Venice, with its heart-stopping beauty and finery, a lifelong passion for Italian style was born.

Matthew's initial adventure with Italianate design began fifteen years ago with the purchase of an early-1920s Italian Revival villa in California. With its broad parterre of low geometric boxwood hedges and five hundred rose bushes, it could have stepped directly from

the pages of Edith Wharton's *Italian Villas and Their Gardens* of 1904. Although of Florentine inspiration, Villa delle Favole also enjoyed the continuity of interior and exterior space so distinctive of Andrea Palladio's Venetian country villas, which are both admired and frequented by Matthew. Having owned a nearby antiques store specializing in Italian objects, Villa delle Favole under his able hands quickly took on the air of a home that had been in the family for centuries. There were paintings and tapestries with their angels and warriors animating the backgrounds, classic and neoclassic sculptures, Venetian blackamoors, and Fortuny toiles.

It was from the Villa delle Favole that Matthew—urged on by his new neighbor Mrs. Dennis (Terry) Stanfill, a founding board member of Save Venice and passionate Italophile—set out on his odyssey with this American organization that restores art and monuments in Venice—and for which he now sits on the board of directors. Save Venice, with its storybook-perfect late-summer adventures that open the barred doors of the Veneto's mythic palaces and villas, brought a new dimension and resonance to Matthew's love affair with Italian style, and he soon found himself giving a masked ball for one hundred and fifty members of the Venetian charity in the villa's tented gardens. (His fellow lover of things Venetian, Elton John, was among the guests.) Some years and many fetes in Venetian palazzi and Palladian villas later, Matthew has designed and built his own neo-Palladian home in the Hudson River valley. On the way, he created great Italianate interiors in two monuments of Italian style in America: first, the palatial, twentieth-century Castle Green, perched in Oriental splendor overlooking Pasadena, California, and an older, American cousin of the Venetian Moorish–style Hotel

Excelsior built on Venice's Lido in 1908; and next, Stanford White's Italian Renaissance Revival building originally known as the J. Hampton and Cornelia Van Rensselaer Robb House in New York.

Matthew transformed the sprawling roof gardens of Castle Green into an at once formal and luxuriantly relaxed Venetian winter garden presided over by a life-size statue of an Etruscan youth standing provocatively at its center, the whole reminiscent of a Luchino Visconti film set where Silvana Mangano might well project her inimitably languid and indolent glamour. Matthew took the two-story, paneled, and coffer-ceilinged former dining room of the Robb mansion in quite an opposite direction, preserving its Belle Epoque grandeur while coaxing it into modern times with great wit and charm.

All the currents of Matthew's love affair with Italian architecture and design come together in his recently built villa Otium in the Hudson Valley.

The front facade of Otium follows the Palladian order of four Doric columns and a pediment, the modified temple portico Palladio introduced early in his career to nobilize and monumentalize the country villas of the Veneto. The broad dome of the interior's central living rotunda is supported by four equal arches. Three are filled by galleries opening to the second story. The fourth forms a proscenium opening to a terrace with a pair of two-story-high Doric columns framing the valley beyond to operatic effect.

However, beyond the romance of Otium, there is a Jamesian "high clearness" in the suave simplification of Palladian architecture and disengagement from detail. There is a certain nobleness in the unassuming authority of the building as it quietly dominates the landscape, and there is a sociable symmetry everywhere. ◼

OPPOSITE Beneath a loggia at Otium, Matthew White's house in the Hudson Valley, New York, stands a stone garden table supporting a bronze deer—a copy of an ancient original discovered in Herculaneum.

OVERLEAF LEFT A nineteenth-century copy of a bust of Augustus is crowned with ivy and adorned with a vintage necklace by Tony Duquette, the great California designer.

OVERLEAF RIGHT The glazed terra-cotta roundel with the head of a lion came from an early-twentieth-century building in Los Angeles but was clearly inspired by antiquity.

INTRODUCTION

IN PURSUIT OF BEAUTY

By Matthew White

The world I inhabit today is in many ways quite different from the world I was born into. At least that seems to be the perception of those who are charmed by appearances. I am a designer, so I understand the allure of appearances. Still, my background, like my earliest dreams, is an essential part of who I was. And who I am today.

I can still picture the neon and metal sign that announced our home in Amarillo, Texas. It was huge and had letters cleverly angled, topsy-turvy style, to suggest the ever-present rolling, dried weeds of the panhandle. TUMBLEWEED TRAILER PARK flashed in glamorous 1950s lettering at the entrance on Grand Avenue. The trailer park was a place my father had built on a flat, dusty parcel of land next to his parents' and grandparents' houses. Within this park was our first home—a fourteen-foot trailer. As our family grew, so did the trailer houses, until the six of us ended up in the ultimate: a double-wide.

The Whites at home. I am the fourth from the top.

There wasn't much around us back then except Leo's Drive-in (best burgers in town) and the bowling alley. Eventually, some truck stops and a motel were built nearby, but mostly the area was dotted with farmhouses, barns, and open fields surrounded by barbed wire fences—the only things capable of stopping the tumbleweeds.

The Tumbleweed Trailer Park, Amarillo, Texas, early 1960s.

Growing up in a trailer park was not exactly a visual feast. The trash cans in front of the tin-clad homes were only partly concealed by cars and picket fences. The lots had small patios and often a clothesline, where clean laundry blew horizontally in the never-ending wind.

There was, however, the occasional retired couple with a neat tool shed filled with gardening tools and fertilizer at the back. One such couple had a pristine turquoise-and-white trailer set in a perfectly manicured garden. They had a birdhouse hanging from a Chinese elm and a birdbath in its shadow. To see their lilacs and daffodils bloom in the springtime was a heavenly sight.

Although these tiny bits of Eden were few and far between, they made a big impression on me. My mother worked hard to improve our garden. Each spring we went to the local nursery to buy flats of petunias and perhaps a climbing rose or two. It was a trip filled with optimism and the delicious anticipation of inevitable beauty.

The impetus for these nursery trips was the ideas we gathered when Mamma drove us through Amarillo's most elegant neighborhoods. My two brothers, my sister, and I would be loaded into the white Chevy, with its fins and blue scratchy interior, and off we'd go in search of escape and inspiration.

To make it an even more special treat, Mamma would stop at Leo's Drive-in on the way. Bags of burgers and onion rings filled the car with a mouthwatering aroma as we each carefully held a red-and-white waxed paper cup of ice-cold root beer or, on a good day, chocolate malts. Then we would continue on our way with Mamma, who is only five feet tall, wrestling the Chevy (without power *anything*) to what we called the Fancy Part of Town.

For Mamma, this was dream time, and it was for me, too. It was like entering a foreign world. The streets were paved in old red brick that rumbled reassuringly under the wheels of our car. Lining these streets were enormous trees that created a canopy of dappled green. Squirrels would frolic there as if they were movie extras paid to create atmosphere. Even the air seemed different, somehow softer, cleaner. It would splash against our faces as we rolled down the windows … and there wasn't a tumbleweed in sight.

The homes were built in the early part of the twentieth century. Set back from the street, each one was perfectly framed by a garden, as if waiting for someone to take its picture. Banks of tulips, crocuses popping up in seeming spontaneity under budding maples, daffodils by the thousands in huge circles of brilliant color. The flawless lawns appeared to be vast plains of emerald green velvet.

The Harrington mansion, Amarillo, Texas.

My favorite house was the Harrington mansion, owned by the oilman Don Harrington and his wife, Sybil. Graced with towering columns, it represented serious Texas money, and plenty of it. The mansion spoke of luxury and permanence—quite a contrast to our house on wheels. This imposing house, like all the ones we admired, was maintained to absolute perfection. The trim seemed to be freshly painted and the windows sparkled, reflecting fragments of garden color—and our passing white Chevy.

I think Mamma felt that the Harrington house was a little over-the-top, but for me it was, in the words of Goldilocks from my storybooks, "just right." As we continued our tour through this rarified world, Mamma would sometimes see a place so beautiful she was forced to pull over so that we could take it all in. We would share what we liked and then drive on, our heads rhythmically moving from side to side.

Although we did not have much, we were not poor. By the Harringtons' standards we might have been considered so, but we had everything we needed. We didn't look at these houses with envy—longing, certainly, but not envy.

As we noisily slurped through our straws the last drops of soda pop and balled up the crinkly paper that had wrapped our devoured hamburgers, Mamma

would sigh. Then with great resolve she would say, "This fall, we'll plant bulbs." Putting all of her ninety-eight pounds into turning the car around, she would take us home.

My fantasy bedroom, incorporating the new bookcase, drawn when I was seven years old.

Mamma's beautification efforts extended to the inside of our trailer house as well. When I was seven, she decorated the bedroom I shared with my older brother, even arranging for a family friend to build us a bookcase. The bookcase was based on her precise drawing and specific measurements. That made a lasting impression on me, the fact that you could create *reality* based on an *idea*.

Previously, my dreams and reality had inhabited very different worlds, but now I saw a way to make them come together. With that concept in mind, I drew how I wanted my room to look, incorporating into the design the new bookcase. It was my first attempt to draw an interior elevation, long before I knew what one even was. On the bookcase, I carefully placed a few books where I could easily reach them. On the upper shelves, I drew vases with flowers. I designed a bed with extravagant finials and created a neat, fitted bedcover on which I placed a doll. At that age (and to the confusion of some), dolls and flowers were unquestionably my favorite things.

Above the bed, I drew a self-portrait depicting myself as a miniature dandy with a scarf tied rakishly around my neck and a big curl centered on my forehead. In order for my room design to appeal to a larger audience, I, rather oddly, drew a gun on the wall and leaned a baseball bat against the bookcase. These were peculiar last-minute additions, as guns and bats didn't interest me in the slightest. While I knew I didn't necessarily want these objects in my room, I remember thinking how clever my placement of them was. The bat, leaning casually against the bookcase, no longer represented sports equipment but became an accessory that added a feeling of spontaneity to the image. Even at seven I was not just designing a room, I was styling it.

The farmhouse.

Three years later, my parents bought a small farmhouse set on five acres directly behind the trailer

park. With a big half-circle drive and plenty of mature trees, the place seemed to me to be quite grand. At the back stood a small barn with a corral surrounded by fields. Off to the side was a little bunkhouse. The surrounding fields were dry and dusty, with native grass, thorny stickers, and horned toads. The stickers were a problem, as I chose to remain barefoot from June to September, but that didn't stop us from playing endlessly out back. We flooded prairie dogs from their holes, flew handmade kites, and caught countless horned toads that, when provoked, would spit blood from their eyes. I never pushed them to such a response, instead preferring to catch the babies who looked like teensy, tiny dinosaurs with white bellies, soft as kid-leather gloves.

It wasn't long before we planted an enormous vegetable garden and a forty-tree orchard. The low-slung barn became a coop for our chickens, two ducks, and a very cranky goose named Lucy. At the mere sight of a child, Lucy would honk and furiously flap her wings, then race in a beeline to bite her chosen victim. It came to the point where we were afraid to go outside. Lucy ended up roasted on our dining room table—an equally unpleasant experience.

Posing with a fishing pole while my brother Joel does the heavy lifting, about 1962.

The corral contained our goats ... most of the time. When they escaped (and they were experts at unlocking gates), they would decimate the flower garden, making mature rose bushes disappear entirely. On more than one occasion we heard our mother's shrieks as she rushed from the kitchen, swinging a dish towel. Her screams were followed by moaning cries as she mourned the loss of her flower bed, yet again.

In spite of its being the dreaded tornado season, spring was my favorite time of year. Not only was it the harbinger of school-less, shoeless days, but it was also a busy time of planting the garden, bringing home fresh batches of impossibly soft yellow chicks, and welcoming new baby goats into the menagerie.

Birthing the goats was a big deal. The first time it happened, Daddy woke us up well after midnight to witness the miracle. The nanny goat was lying on her side on a bed of hay in the garage, her enormous stomach bulging. Above, a bare lightbulb illuminated the scene. As she bleated in obvious pain, her eyes would dramatically roll back in her head. Daddy was busy assisting and told us to come and stand near him to watch. As we stood there in our robes, a hoof emerged and soon a baby slid out, slippery as stewed okra. Then another! In mere minutes, they raised up on shaky legs and tender hoofs. We *loved* them and could barely sleep through the night in anticipation of seeing them again the next morning.

The perpetual motion of baby goats.

After a few days, Daddy weaned them off their mother so that we could take her milk. As we bottle-fed the newborns, we developed a deep bond with them, and they with us.

The twin kids were the image

of youthful exuberance. They followed us everywhere. They would, well ... *frolic*—that's the only word to describe their antics. They would prance and run, kick up their heels, and then, without warning, jump high into the air. Once aloft, they seemed to hover, then jangle in a spastic dance of sheer joy. After the unlikely aerial display, they would land soft as kittens, never missing a beat as they scampered on behind us. They were heaven.

The first few years we lived in the two-bedroom farmhouse, I shared a room with my three siblings—but we were getting bigger. It was decided that my brother and I would move into the bunkhouse, while my sister and youngest brother remained in our old room.

Mamma began preparing the bunkhouse by selecting pale green paint from Sears. After painting, she made curtains in a textured fabric a shade darker than the walls. Deep-blue-and-green plaid bedspreads from J.C. Penney completed the scheme. We dubbed the little house "the boys' room."

"The boys' room" is in the background at right.

I was excited about the boys' room because it took my love of domesticity to an entirely new level. Rather than simply a *room,* we had an entire *house.* It wasn't long before I took ownership of the place. I started by planting zinnias and morning glories and carefully mowing the surrounding lawn, cutting precise stripes with the wheels of the lawnmower. I even sunk a discarded bathtub into the ground, centering it squarely on direct axis of the back door to

create a miniature reflecting pool. I had very grand ideas and, in my head, was designing my "estate."

It was then that I started paying more attention to the design magazines Mamma subscribed to. Reading about Billy Baldwin or Albert Hadley and seeing the rooms they created opened my eyes to possibilities I hadn't realized existed. I learned new words like *enfilade* and *treillage* and inspected every photograph as if it held a secret code. Of course, each photo *did* hold countless secrets, and I made it my business to decipher them.

My bedroom, drawn when I was sixteen years old.

Around that time, Mamma gave me a copy of *Billy Baldwin Decorates,* my first interior design book. I devoured it, rereading it over and over again. I used the boys' room as a laboratory, constantly moving things around to discover the best possible effect. Out in the world, I would find discarded pieces and then transform them with a coat of paint or a scrap of fabric. These "new" pieces would be put into the mix, allowing me to reevaluate everything and see the entire room with fresh eyes. These experiments taught me about scale, proportion, and balance. I learned how one piece could change the entire landscape of a room. I had no money to spend on those efforts; it was all assembled with

Texas gumption and elbow grease.

One afternoon, Mamma and Daddy sat us all down to tell us about a very big change coming our way. We were told that when they married, their big dream was to be missionaries in China. But because Daddy had a hearing problem, he didn't pass the physical. Now, more than a decade later, with four kids, he had been accepted to assist in mission work in Mexico for one school year. Daddy was to teach the children of Bible translators. So off we went to our new life in Old Mexico.

With our travel trailer and Chevy station wagon packed, we waved good-bye to our extended family, who would manage the trailer park in our absence. Our destination—and our home for the next nine months—would be the tiny town of Ixmiquilpan, in the state of Hidalgo, just an hour's drive north of Mexico City. After four days of driving, we arrived at last to find the town, nestled in a fertile valley of alfalfa and corn fields surrounded by huge maguey plants. As we drove into the heart of Ixmiquilpan, we saw a large fountain in the center of the town square. If we hadn't realized before that we were in a foreign country, we certainly did when we saw the huge, and shockingly nude, statue of Diana the Huntress surmounting the fountain. There she was, right out in the open for all to see.

On one corner of the plaza stood a church built around 1550. It seemed impossibly old, given that my previous impression of an old building was the Harrington house back home, built in 1913. The interior of the church had soaring Gothic arches, while the walls were frescoed with strange scenes of violence—jaguar warriors and eagle men fighting an ancient war with centaurs. Foliate designs created a background for seminude warriors with plumed helmets and pregnant women emerging from giant blossoms. I didn't realize these were unusual images for a Catholic church, since anything Catholic was very exotic to us. The whole idea of art in a church was something I had never even considered as a possibility. Our church back home had plain, painted cinder-block walls and an acoustical ceiling. The church in Ixmiquilpan, by contrast, was built so that as soon as one entered, there was no question that it was an exalted place.

Matthew in Ixmiquilpan, Mexico, in 1970.

We lived in a compound one mile from the center of town. Inside the walled campus stood a small, flat-roofed church, a dozen single-story houses, and a school. With our new schoolmates leading

the pack, we would escape the compound to eat tacos from street vendors, sneak into the hidden rooms of the old Catholic church, or skinny-dip in the shockingly polluted Rio Tula. These were all forbidden pleasures, of course, making us feel like Tom Sawyer on a trip *way* down south. Snooping around the church was especially exciting. Inside, we would find storerooms stacked high with centuries-old, glassy-eyed saints dressed in vestments that glistened with gold thread. Most often, we were to be found in the bell tower, ringing the heavy bronze bells as the sleepy, sunbaked town went about its business below.

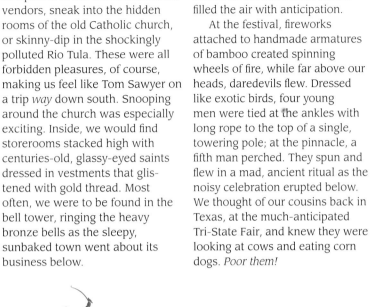

Ixmiquilpan town square, with the nude Diana and a Catholic church in the background.

In October, Ixmiquilpan started preparing for the fabulously macabre *Día de los Muertos*, or Day of the Dead. During the weeks leading up to the festivities, it seemed as though every Mexican man, woman, and child worked on the preparations and decor. They made thousands of elaborately attired skeletons ranging in size from miniature to mammoth. Ladies would gather to sweep the cemeteries clean, then the graves were laden with mounds of marigolds, some woven into elaborate designs. The yellow-orange flowers glowed with

intensity against the gray tombstones as the acrid floral aroma filled the air with anticipation.

At the festival, fireworks attached to handmade armatures of bamboo created spinning wheels of fire, while far above our heads, daredevils flew. Dressed like exotic birds, four young men were tied at the ankles with long rope to the top of a single, towering pole; at the pinnacle, a fifth man perched. They spun and flew in a mad, ancient ritual as the noisy celebration erupted below. We thought of our cousins back in Texas, at the much-anticipated Tri-State Fair, and knew they were looking at cows and eating corn dogs. *Poor them!*

On Friday afternoons we would hop in the Chevy for weekend excursions, always looking like gringos and being viewed as impossibly rich by the locals (that was a switch!). We'd see Mayan ruins and Spanish colonial villages. Or Daddy would navigate seemingly endless, smog-choked freeways into the vast urban center of Mexico City, where we'd visit the Museo Nacional de Antropología, the elegant shops of the Zona Rosa, or the Thieves' Market.

Everywhere we went we saw poverty the likes of which I never knew existed. Those images were

contrasted with scenes of tremendous visual poetry. That Christmas, when school was closed, we took an extended trip, driving all the way to the Guatemalan border. It was after dark on Christmas Eve when we happened upon an ancient church glowing with a thousand candles. The monumental doors had been thrown wide open, allowing music and the crush of worshippers to spill out. It was the most ravishing thing I had ever seen, causing spontaneous tears to swell in my eyes.

Mexico was filled with visual and emotional experiences that were more than I could take in and fully comprehend. I was too painfully shy to speak Spanish well, but words were never my world. I soaked in the experience of Mexico through my eyes and returned to Texas with a much-expanded view.

Back at home, and now a year older, my brother and I would work beside our father at Tumbleweed Park. The trailer park was a real family business, and we did everything from trimming trees and mowing lawns to picking up the trash and dealing with stopped-up sewers.

These disagreeable chores were tempered by outside pursuits, one being music. We all began piano lessons at a very young age and were expected by our parents to keep it up through our high school graduation. But it wasn't until I returned from Mexico that these lessons started to resonate.

Our teacher, Millicent Lahm, taught me much more than playing the piano. She imbued our lessons with a historic perspective that incorporated art and the great places of Europe. As a young lady in the late 1910s, she had studied in Vienna and traveled to Italy. She allowed me to look through her old albums loaded with photographs of her grand tour.

Toward the end of high school, I landed a job delivering furniture for Hughes Home Beautiful, the finest furniture store in town. The shop was small, with two decorators on staff. Store vignettes were changed regularly, so when I wasn't making deliveries (to the grand houses I was driven past as a child), I worked with the designers, moving pieces around the shop to suit their vision. It wasn't long before I felt comfortable making suggestions, and in no time I was having a much larger impact on the window displays and vignettes. Eventually, I was allowed to design some displays on my own.

Hughes Home Beautiful, Amarillo, Texas.

At Hughes, dressed for success, 1976.

Creating store displays was just like rearranging my room, but with better furniture. The experience led to a newfound confidence, which inspired me to redecorate my own space in the boys' room. Like Mamma, I started by going to Sears to buy cans of paint, this time in deep red. I then found sheets that I would use to make curtains and bolsters. Of course I had my own sewing machine (what sixteen-year-old boy didn't?). At the store, I splurged and ordered a few yards of highly polished cotton to make throw pillows. I painted the bookcase that Mamma built for us

many years before, and then I used a matchstick blind to cover the lower shelves, where I stored less-attractive necessities.

My redecorated room, 1976.

The red bedroom with the bookcase.

Around this time, my parents wanted to add an entrance hall to the main house, so Daddy asked me to design it. Design a room from the ground up? In a *heartbeat*! In no time I drew up a tall, elegant addition with a mansard roof and a front door flanked by fluted pilasters and brass lanterns. For the inside I created a tray ceiling to reflect the exterior shape.

For the interior decoration, I chose overscale, green-and-white fretwork wallpaper to make the room feel like a garden pavilion. From the ceiling I hung a simple brass and glass lantern. The curtains on the one tall window were made of a highly polished cotton chintz with bright yellow birds in a verdant garden. Rather than a console table, my mother wanted a desk so that the room could double as her office. I chose a white lacquered desk with faux-bamboo details and a white,

tooled-leather top. To me, this foyer was the height of elegance. What it was doing stuck onto a Texas farmhouse is another question entirely.

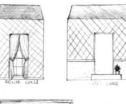

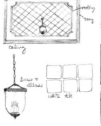

BEFORE AFTER

Elevations and exterior shots of the entry hall added to our farmhouse in 1976.

That was the year I graduated from high school and, after saving my money from the two prior years, I went to Europe. It was a tour of Eastern Europe, arranged through the German and Russian language classes of my cousin's high school in Oregon. I was the Texas interloper, ruthlessly teased for my twangy accent, a trait I lost without even trying over the course of the forty-day trip.

Germany, Switzerland, Holland, Denmark, and the Soviet Union were all on the itinerary. I saw things I had only dreamed of—Russian palaces, Roman ruins, Rembrandts. I came home transfigured. My idea of what was beautiful, first brought into focus in Mexico, had now been informed by Europe. I had a deep hunger to see more.

While I was forging my path to becoming an interior designer, a new passion had suddenly surfaced: dance. At sixteen, I saw my first ballet when the Lone Star Ballet of Amarillo performed *The Nutcracker* with guest artists from the legendary New York City Ballet. I don't think I blinked a single time after the curtain went up.

The Nutcracker blended my love of classical music with dreamlike visuals. It was a study in form, atmospheric effect, and expressive movement, all seamlessly inter-twining with Tchaikovsky's score. I was done for.

A year later, my sister, who had been studying ballet, was cast in the production. Since they needed boys, she volunteered me to be a walk-on. I was cast in fairly simple parts—a parent, a mouse, and a veil-bearing slave to an Arabian princess. I was at every rehearsal, watching. That was my first glimpse behind the looking glass.

The rehearsal studio was a place of hard work and appreciated effort, all geared toward one thing: the performance.

On opening night, when the overture started and the curtain went up, it was like living in a dream, all while being acutely aware of reality. Onstage, one is conscious of its inner workings. Outfitted in full costume and makeup, with music swelling all around, I stood in front of the painted sets. Above my head and in the wings were a million lights and endless activity. Dancers fidgeted as they waited for their entrance while stagehands manipulated ropes and pulleys to produce the effects of growing trees and falling snow. Before me was a vast darkness, as the orchestra created a rising waterfall of music. The audience was in an entirely different realm, sitting on the other side and perceptible only by sound. I used to be one of them, but now I stood where the magic was being made.

In the ballet studio, 1980.

That blending of real and imagined worlds was one I felt very comfortable in. By its nature, the theater is presentational, so it was enormously appealing to me. Each moment was meticulously rehearsed to create that instant of enchantment, the splendid reveal. I started taking ballet classes and learned I had a natural ability.

Performing in the Los Angeles Ballet production of The Nutcracker, *1982.*

The fork in the road was before me: I had to choose whether to pursue ballet seriously or to regret forever not trying. That year I auditioned for the summer program at the School of American Ballet in New York City. A

month later, the fateful letter arrived. It probably wasn't easy for my parents to accept their son's pursuing a career as a professional dancer, but they never once questioned my choice. With their loving support, I headed to New York, where I worked in an antiques shop to offset expenses.

New York was a big change from Amarillo, but I had been to Mexico City, Berlin, Moscow, and other great cities, so I had a good idea of what I would be facing. On my first day I saw the final performance of the New York City Ballet's spring season, which closed with George Balanchine's spectacular *Symphony in C*. It was eye-popping—the speed of the first movement, the heart-stopping music of the adagio, and the spectacle of a company of dancers sparkling like jewels in a glorious crown.

The school had a very different glamour. It was a place of hushed hallways cluttered with willowy dancers, pale and exotic. As we took class, Russian women would evaluate our every move, then whisper, point, and jot down notes in a book. It was a strange world, very American and yet a product of the *ancien régime*. The formality and manners expected

of the students in class were steeped in centuries of the French royal court and imperial Russia. The experience was both alluring and nerve-racking. Without warning, George Balanchine and Lincoln Kirstein would casually walk in to observe class, which would cause my heart nearly to stop. I might have just fallen off the turnip truck, but I knew I was in the presence of genius.

I left the School of American Ballet to study with the great ballerina Melissa Hayden, and a year later I was hired to join the Los Angeles Ballet. I was just twenty and had already realized what many had thought was an impossible dream.

When I was twenty-three, the Los Angeles Ballet hired a new assistant general manager, the equally young Thomas Schumacher. Tom, a theater major fresh from the University of California, Los Angeles, entered my professional life, and while he didn't notice me among the many dancers in the company, I had definitely noticed him.

I have always been good at assessing quality, not only in objects but also in people. It was clear to me that Tom was very special. I soon learned he had a strong character, a great sense of humor, and values I admired. In no time, we became an item, and soon after, he moved in.

Thomas and Matthew in their first apartment, painted by Jorge Vargas in 1983.

With the exception of super-stars like Rudolf Nureyev, ballet dancers weren't known to live in

grand style. But I was able to pay my own expenses and make small purchases for the apartment, at one point even springing for a used baby grand piano.

Tom was always, *always* working. While managing the Los Angeles Ballet, he had irons in several other fires, all related to the theater. But even so, our combined income was meager. A few years into our relationship, we took our first vacation, a road trip to Northern California to visit a tiny mountain cabin owned by his Italian grandmother. It was a great trip, but on the drive home we talked about our dream vacation. Tom had never been to Europe, and I was eager to see Italy and France. I suggested that if we each saved twenty dollars a week, then in a year or two we would have enough money to take a *real* trip. We started saving that week.

One of the places Tom moon-lighted at was the Mark Taper Forum, Los Angeles' major theater. That led to his becoming a line producer for the theater component of the groundbreaking Los Angeles Olympic Arts Festival, part of the 1985 Olympic Games. The festival, an enormous artistic and financial success, created a surplus that would fund a biennial arts event called, simply, the Los Angeles Festival.

In order to curate the various international theater, music, and dance companies, Tom was required to travel to see their work. His first international trip was to attend the Festival d'Avignon, and so our first European adventure together was decided for us. We loved France, but we both agreed that our next trip would be to Italy, so the saving continued.

Within a year, we finally made it. Italy *at last*! Our budget was by no stretch a large one, but we were able to spend two weeks in the big three—Rome, Florence, and Venice. We started in Rome, and before we had even unpacked, we were out on the street. The Pantheon was the first great monument we entered—not a bad place to begin one's grand tour. But then, with so much to take in on one's first trip to Italy, it is difficult to make a wrong move. We devoured Rome and Florence, our breath taken away at every turn. Then came Venice.

The first time I saw Venice, Italy, 1986.

It was from a train that late September evening when we first laid eyes on Venice. Night was falling, and our view through the window as we crossed the lagoon made the city appear as a sleeping giant lying thin and elegant on the water. I knew I would love Venice long before we had even begun to plan the trip, long before I arrived there. Venice represented, to me, a city from a different realm. A place really not of this world. How else could one explain a city of

stone palaces built on water?

Finally, the train stopped, and out we stepped to the Grand Canal, water lapping at our feet. We had carefully written the name of our vaporetto stop on a folded piece of paper, along with the words *Pensione Wildner*, a place that was secured on our behalf months before by our good friend Robert Fitzpatrick. No Gritti Palace for us, and no Hotel Danieli—we were traveling on a shoestring.

The city was cloaked in silence. As we glided down the Grand Canal, I looked up at the darkened palaces. The ancient facades glowed in the moonlight. Once in a great while, a piano nobile would show signs of life, glowing like a beacon in a sleeping city. Windows thrown open to take in the late summer air allowed muffled conversation or music to waft over the water. These lit rooms granted us glimpses of ceilings that groaned under the weight of sculpted plaster figures supporting vast, celestial paintings. I felt like the outsider's outsider, with my mouth agape and a suitcase at my feet. I looked up at these rooms illuminated by enormous chandeliers made centuries earlier in this very city. They didn't sparkle like the crystal chandeliers of Paris— the Venetian chandeliers *glimmered*. They glimmered with a dim

luster like the inky water that held us aloft as we floated into the heart of my dream city.

The next morning, we threw open the shutters of our simple room, unleashing light so relentless and blinding that it felt as though we were inside a prism. After arriving in darkness the night before, we were shocked to see the glinting lagoon and, beyond that, the Lido. We were dazzled by the crystal blue sky and its shattered reflection where the ground should have been. This sparkling ground danced to the rhythm of the boats.

Out amid our fellow tourists, we ventured to discover the treasures of Venice. We hit the usual suspects, but none were what one could call usual: the magnificent, gilt-edged monumentality of the rooms in the Doge's Palace, the undulating inlaid marble floors and gilded mosaic domes of the Basilica di San Marco. But eventually our trip came to an end. Pulling ourselves away from Italy was difficult, but I returned home knowing that Venice had awakened something deep inside me.

I had stopped dancing not long before our Italian tour. The company was having financial problems, and I had suffered a few minor injuries. Like most dancers, I knew the clock was ticking. I decided it was time to move on. After years of dancing, I was far removed from the world of interior design and, frankly, a little intimidated by it. I knew my high school job creating store windows would impress no one. So I went back to school to become a graphic designer. At the time it felt like a more serious career choice.

A few years later, after producing the inaugural Los Angeles Festival, Tom was hired by Walt Disney Studios to produce his first animated film, *The Rescuers Down Under*. This was before the resurgence of animation, so, to the shock of our theater friends, he

took a pay *cut* from his prior job in the nonprofit sector to work for a major Hollywood studio.

Just as Tom was starting his job at Disney, we bought our first house. It was a 1915 Arts and Crafts bungalow in a historic Pasadena neighborhood—a complete and utter wreck. Every surface was caked, camouflaged, or coated in horrifying finishes or inappropriate materials, all amateurishly applied. Windows were boarded over, as was a gaping hole in the floor.

Sweat equity in Pasadena, California, 1989.

Our first house, fully restored, 1992.

Tom grew up in a household where the idea of hanging a picture was considered major construction, so renovation was a bit overwhelming to him at first. I, however, thrived on creating transformation.

Our willing construction companion, Phoebe.

We didn't have the budget to hire a contractor, so we took on that role ourselves. In fact, we did most of the actual work ourselves, replacing or redoing every single surface inside and out. Every day after work, I would pick up our eager basset hound, Phoebe, and speed to the house, where we would rip, strip, and scrape until midnight. Weekends were spent entirely at the house, slowly putting it in proper order. After a few months, our house of horrors became clean and livable, and we made the big move.

Within a year, we turned the previously sad little house into a monument to the power of good choices and hard work.

The joy of the transformation highlighted the fact that I was stagnating in the two-dimensional world of typefaces and page layouts as a graphic designer. I craved a chance to work in the three-dimensional world I loved. On weekends, I discovered estate sales and flea markets in Pasadena, and due to my weakness for antiques, I soon opened a booth at the local market.

My business grew, and I eventually stopped working as a graphic designer so that I could open Matthew White Antiques and Interiors. Although I didn't have a single design client, it wasn't long before people responded to how I put things together. In short order, I developed a following. Mine was a rather indirect path back to the world of interior design, but at long last I had found my way.

We sold the bungalow and continued to restore old houses, each one becoming a bit larger and more directly influenced by Italy. At my shop, I sold pieces from a broad spectrum of periods and cultures, the only thing tying the objects together was that they appealed to my eye. But the Italian pieces, with their theatricality and charm, touched me most. Those were the pieces I brought home.

The Villa delle Favole—a fantasy realized.

I eventually gave up the shop to concentrate solely on design. By this time, we had started renovating an Italian revival villa in San Marino, California, which we called the Villa delle Favole—the "House of Myths and Fairytales."

It was while living at the Villa delle Favole that I met our neighbors and dear friends Terry and Dennis Stanfill. Terry introduced me to Save Venice, an American organization that restores art and monuments in the magical city. After learning more about Save Venice, I decided to host a fund-raiser in our garden and started laying the plans for an extravagant masked ball. Tastemakers, jet-setters, socialites, and rock stars attended—it was an unqualified success.

My event launched the newly formed California Chapter, headed by Terry Stanfill and co-chaired by Hutton Wilkinson and me. Because of these efforts, I was invited to be a trustee on the board of directors.

At Disney, Tom had produced the movie *The Lion King* and then became the president of Feature Animation. After ultimately overseeing more animated films than Walt Disney himself, Tom co-produced the Broadway production of *The Lion King* with his business partner, Peter Schneider. Finally, he left animation and began producing musicals full-time. Like me, Tom had found the path back to *his* first love, the theater. Producing shows on Broadway made having a house in California no longer practical, so we moved to New York.

Once we were settled in Manhattan, I met my future business partner, Frank Webb, since he happened to live in our building. Frank and I connected over our contrasting but compatible decorating styles and joined forces professionally and creatively to form White Webb, an interior design firm.

Matthew and Thomas at the Villa delle Favole.

This book is not about the varied client projects of White Webb. Instead, it is an expression of my personal style and its inspiration. In these pages, I share how I was seduced by Italy and how that seduction has affected the style in which *I* live. Just as the grand tour so deeply affected travelers three hundred years ago, Italy continues to move and inspire me. So within these pages is my grand tour of sorts, a tour of my Italian-inspired homes past and present. Each one of these houses, whether situated in town or in the country, on the East or the West Coast, links three essential elements: a love of domesticity, a love of beauty, and a love of Italy.

There's an old Tuscan proverb, "Man makes the place, and the place makes the man." From my earliest days at the trailer park, the greatest joy of my life has been the pursuit of beauty. I found it most profoundly in Italy, but I have been blessed to create it at home. ▧

"There was no citizen ... who was not in the process of building ... a handsome dwelling ... much better than in the city. It was such a magnificent sight that those coming from outside and not familiar with Florence believed that the fine buildings and beautiful palaces in a three-mile band outside the town made it a Roman-style city." —Giovanni Villani, Cronica, *around 1340*

The ancient Italian villa was a grand house built outside the city walls and took a variety of forms. The type known as *villa urbana* was a splendid suburban estate located within easy travel of the city. These were generally pleasure houses, where one could escape the city during the sweltering summer months. The *villa rustica,* on the other hand, was a working farm owned by a gentleman farmer and usually located farther from town. Whether these ancient villas were surrounded by pleasure gardens or agriculture, they all had one thing in common: They were opulent dwellings outside of the city and owned by citizens of high rank. These villas often had enough land to make the house self-sustaining, with olive groves, vineyards, gardens, and woods for hunting.

OPPOSITE The fifteenth-century Villa di Poggio a Caiano, outside of Florence, was once owned by Lorenzo the Magnificent.

The Renaissance villa in Tuscany has its roots in Roman culture. Roman engineering made it possible for water to be moved by aqueducts, a technology that, when combined with the wealth of the empire, led to the development of elaborate gardens. Roman gardens were famous for their fountains, clipped boxwood, and roses—things many now think of as French or English ideas. But the Romans had invented the first great pleasure gardens in Europe long before there was any power in France or England to create such splendor.

Pliny the Elder (A.D. 23–79) wrote eloquently about many things, including gardens and houses. His surviving letters give us a glimpse into the life that was lived within the great Roman country houses. He spoke of the relationship between the house and its garden and how the garden is really an architectural idea—an extension of the villa. His words,

fifteen hundred years later, inspired Renaissance designers to take gardening beyond the style of the more practical medieval garden to create verdant spaces of visual delight. These ideas spread through Europe and continue to shape garden design today.

Pliny's descriptions of his gardens spark the imagination and show us the great pleasure he took in creating and living in his country estates. Pliny the Younger (circa A.D. 61–113) also had a deep love for his villas and especially his gardens. One of his many villas was in Tuscany.

In the fifth century, after the fall of Rome, there was a long period in Italy and throughout Europe when small fiefdoms were constantly at war. This unsettled atmosphere made it necessary for the great country houses to be armed fortresses rather than places of exterior beauty. It would be more than a thousand years, and well into the Renaissance, before the

"The greater part of the house has a southern aspect and enjoys the afternoon sun in summer and gets it rather later in the winter. It is fronted by a broad and proportionally long colonnade, in front of which is a terrace edged with box and shrubs cut into different shapes. From the terrace you descend by an easy slope to a lawn, and on each side of the descent are figures of animals in box facing each other. You then come to a pleasance formed of soft acanthus. Here also there is a walk bordered by topiary work, and farther on there is an oval space set about with box hedges and dwarf trees." —Pliny the Elder, A.D. FIRST CENTURY

villa would again emerge as a house that embraced the landscape with outward-facing loggias, terraces, and gardens. Florentines during the Renaissance had a great admiration for antiquity. Their desire to emulate what they found through archaeological discoveries is shown in the art and architecture of the age. The Renaissance country house, like its Roman antecedent, was either a place where the nobility could escape the stress and heat of the city, or a working farm with groves and vineyards. The wealthier the family, the more likely it was that their villa was surrounded by formal pleasure gardens with clipped boxwood, statuary, fountains, and potted fruit trees, all laid out in ordered symmetry.

But the Renaissance villa was not only about the garden—the house itself became an important expression of the aspirations of these Florentine families. Vast rooms with cool tile floors and beautifully frescoed walls and ceilings were filled with furnishings and artwork worthy of the owner's social standing. The exteriors were plastered stone, while hipped, red terra-cotta roofs defined the overall form. Loggias provided shady places from which to enjoy the gardens.

Inevitably, a family crest was prominently on display to advertise the importance of the bloodline. The Medici family had many such villas, and they certainly understood the precedent set by their Roman ancestors. One of these villas was the Villa di Poggio a Caiano.

Il Poggio, which still stands about ten miles west of Florence, was purchased by Lorenzo the Magnificent in the second half of the fifteenth century. Immediately, the villa underwent improvements, and except for the double staircase and Baroque clock, the

exterior looks today much as it did during the Renaissance. The pediment over the front loggia may have been a rather incongruous addition, but it shows the desire to create a link with the classical world. It is no surprise that the Medici crest is the central decorative element within this pediment.

Il Poggio was a favorite villa of the Medici clan, and during their time there, they lavished the interiors with decoration. These improvements were carried out by well-known architects and painters of the period, including Fra Filippo Lippi, Andrea del Sarto, Bartolomeo Ammanati, and Alessandro Allori. The gardens, now sadly gone, were no doubt a stunning display of Renaissance symmetry, emulating the storied gardens of antiquity. Il Poggio and various other great Tuscan houses would inspire architects, artists, and writers for centuries. Edith Wharton wrote the book *Italian Villas and Their Gardens* as a way to share her enthusiasm for these romantic places. Bernard Berenson, the famous art historian who specialized in the Italian Renaissance, lived in a charming villa in Fiesole, just outside of Florence. These nineteenth- and early-twentieth-century American tastemakers understood the architectural importance of the Italian country house and were in part responsible for bringing that understanding to a larger audience in the modern age.

Instead of diminishing with time, the charm and romance of the Tuscan villa continues to grow, unlike the once-verdant gardens that live only in the memories of these noble houses. ▥

LEFT The Villa di Poggio a Caiano and its gardens were depicted in a late-sixteenth-century painting by Giusto Utens.

IZCAYA

AN AMERICAN HOMAGE TO THE ITALIAN RENAISSANCE

While many Americans of the late nineteenth and early twentieth centuries were enamored of French or English style of the eighteenth century, some were moved by the romance of Italy. This was especially true in Florida and California, where Mediterranean Revival became a serious architectural movement. The light and terrain of these sunnier states reminded people of Italy, so rather than construct homes influenced by the grayer climates of France or England, architects turned toward Italy and Spain.

Although Addison Mizner was a notable practitioner of the Italian Revival style, perhaps no American house during this period came closer to realizing the idea of the great villas of Italy than did James Deering's Vizcaya, in Miami, Florida. This astonishing house, surrounded by elaborate gardens and positioned directly on Biscayne Bay, recalls the Tuscan villa at its most exuberant. Designed by the young New York painter Paul Chalfin, with F. Burrall Hoffman as the architect and Diego Suarez as the landscape architect, Vizcaya was completed in 1916.

It was originally a nearly one-hundred-and-eighty-acre property, and like all of Italy's great villas, it was surrounded by formal pleasure gardens and agriculture. In this case, the estate had a dairy farm, stables, and greenhouses. But the Renaissance-inspired gardens, laid out in splendid symmetry and lavished with fountains and statuary, are still perhaps what Vizcaya is most famous for.

These gardens include an elaborate man-made breakwater in the form of a stone barge, complete with statues of sea monsters and mermaids. This is the introduction to the villa from the water. On terra firma, the formal gardens are dotted with obelisks and statuary. A teahouse and a casino (pleasure house) give the effect of fabulous garden follies, while fountains, terraces, balustrades, and grand staircases draw one through the gardens.

The house itself is based on the classic Renaissance model, with exterior walls of plaster and stone for quoins and door and window surrounds. So much coral stone was required that Deering purchased a nearby quarry to supply the material. The simplicity of the hipped roof in traditional red terra-cotta completes the picture. Rather than making new roof tiles or exporting antique ones from Italy, old tiles were procured in nearby Cuba and shipped to Florida.

Incorporated into the house are antique remnants taken from palaces and villas in Venice, Rome, and Milan, as well as from French chateaus. The rooms pay homage to nearly five centuries of European design.

Adorning the interiors, loggias, and courtyards is an endless trove of antique elements including a ceiling from the Palazzo de' Rossi in Bologna and monumental iron gates from a palazzo in Venice. Room after room fuses these treasures into a seamless whole. Furnishings are equally rich, with period pieces from Italy, France, Spain, and England. The Renaissance banquet hall is dominated by an Italian tapestry woven in 1550 for Ercole II, Duke of Ferrara, and the room is furnished with an Italian sideboard and chairs from the fifteenth and sixteenth centuries.

Deering's Vizcaya is a fantasy realized. Now, as a museum, it preserves a sumptuous example of one American's interpretation of grand Italian style. ▪

LEFT James Deering's Vizcaya, completed in Miami, Florida, in 1916, is perhaps the most exuberant American example of architecture and gardens inspired by the Renaissance villas of Florence, Italy.

ILLA DELLE FAVOLE

CALIFORNIA MEDITERRANEAN

In 1903, Henry E. Huntington purchased an old ranchero adjacent to Pasadena, California. This vast estate was combined with two others in 1913 to become the city of San Marino. Named after the republic of San Marino in Italy, its first mayor was General George S. Patton Sr.

Henry Huntington felt that Southern California represented America's future, and to prove his commitment, he and his wife, Arabella, began building a grand house on his new estate. The mansion was designed to hold Mr. Huntington's impressive and ever-expanding collection of rare books, fine furniture, and English portraiture. Extensive gardens were planned to hold his collection of exotic botanical specimens.

Construction of the Huntington mansion commenced in 1910 with an army of men who would turn the old ranchero into a palatial residence inspired by the grand houses of Europe. Among the legions of workers was a young apprentice named Joe Weston, a fifteen-year-old boy who dreamed of one day becoming an architect. In 1914, he left California and began his studies in Philadelphia, at the University of Pennsylvania, and in 1915 became an apprentice at Atelier Hirons, a Beaux-Arts architectural firm in New York City.

Weston, along with his younger brother Eugene, was a seeker of adventure and a lover of beauty. Whether he was traveling on horseback from Los Angeles to San Diego to see the California missions or sketching on the roof of the atelier in New York, Joe could always be found sketching. He was an extremely gifted draftsman and would study the smallest detail of a cornice or doorknob. While in New York, he was often found at the Metropolitan Museum of Art with sketchpad in hand, making studies of Renaissance furniture or period architectural details.

American architects of this period were products of the Beaux-Arts school, and the Weston brothers were no different. Architects in California, however, also had the beautiful, romantic California missions from which to draw inspiration. Built in the eighteenth and early nineteenth centuries, these much-admired structures created a vision of what California had been and what it would become. Just a century before San Marino became a city, the land it occupied was a part of the San Gabriel Mission. El Molino Viejo, "the Old Mill," built around 1816, still stands near the Huntington estate and acts as a testament to these earlier days in old *Californio*. The simple forms of these unpretentious, elegant buildings suited both the strong light and the mild climate.

In this new part of the New World, there was a desire to shake off the old influences of the East Coast. As the Victorian era became a memory, one could find no better place to reinvent oneself than California. Many of these new residents saw an opportunity to start fresh, without falling back on the expected Anglo-American architectural influences of the past. Although the Mediterranean style may have been inspired by the past, it was not a past known by most Americans, so for many it represented an exotic "new" style.

"There's never a new fashion but it's old." —Geoffrey Chaucer

In California during the early 1920s, the building boom was heating up to a fevered pitch, and the Mediterranean style was all the rage. As more people relocated to the Golden State, they increasingly wanted this lovely, romantic vision of what California represented.

In the early 1920s, the Weston brothers opened their architectural offices in Los Angeles, and not long afterward, Mr. and Mrs. Tom Kester commissioned an Italian-style house to be built in San Marino. Kester was an advertising man whose primary client was the fruit industry. His lovely wife, Maude, was an enthusiastic decorator who loved to entertain. Their new villa, built in 1924, was obviously created to hold beautiful parties.

The Kesters' garden was small compared to the vast botanical gardens of the nearby Huntington mansion, but the couple created a verdant space of great elegance and charm. Years before, when Kester was just nineteen, he worked as a journeyman on a restoration project at Mount Vernon, Virginia. During this time, he visited Gunston Hall, his cousin's nearby home. This grand plantation house, with its old boxwood garden, clearly made an impression on the young man.

It has recently been discovered that Gunston Hall has Virginia's oldest known boxwood shrubs, dating from the mid-eighteenth century. In Colonial America, the great houses of prosperous colonies nearly always included pleasure gardens inspired by those of Europe. Formal European gardens were based on the Renaissance model, which descended from ancient Roman gardens. When Kester built his California villa, many years after visiting Gunston Hall, he insisted on including an elaborate boxwood parterre. Whether he was aware of it or not, he surrounded his Italian-style house with a garden whose roots were Italian as well.

The Kester house was inspired by the Renaissance villas of Tuscany. The most alluring space in the house, and the only surviving interior, was the library. Here, the Weston brothers conceived the perfect marriage of house and garden. By using an unusual tile on the floor of the library and its adjoining courtyard, the Westons created the ideal example of indoor-outdoor living. Separating these two spaces was a wall of leaded glass that gave the room a modern sense of openness, even though it was crafted with a centuries-old technique. And just like the great families of Italy had done before her, Mrs. Kester incorporated her family crest into the design of the leaded glass. Against one wall of the courtyard, Eugene Weston designed a stunning tiled-wall fountain especially for this space and signed it with the Weston mark.

Over the years, and with the exception of the library, many changes were made to the house's interiors—some quite drastic. Mrs. Kester was constantly redecorating, later adding French-style moldings and fireplaces. In the 1940s, she installed a Lucite and aluminum stair railing. Because of these changes and those of later owners, the interiors fell victim to current fashions, removing any link to the Tuscan-style exterior.

The Italian-style parterre, however, remained miraculously intact. In the 1980s, a pool and a pool house were added in the lower garden. Mark Berry, a noted California landscape architect, understood the style of the house and, with great sensitivity, designed the pool to perfectly complement the original garden. In spite of these many changes over the decades, the house has retained its lovely facade, and the library and courtyard have remained the soul of the house. Even though the garden in past years was sadly neglected, the essence of its Renaissance style has endured.

OPPOSITE The California architect Joe Weston, 1915, sketching on a New York rooftop as an apprentice for the architectural firm Atelier Hirons.

ABOVE RIGHT The San Marino, California, villa belonging to Mr. and Mrs. Tom Kester was photographed around 1923, when it was still under construction.

RIGHT Olive trees and a sprawling California live oak frame the Tuscan-inspired Kester villa in a photograph taken in the late 1920s.

When I first saw the house, it conjured a specific image. I imagined a gleaming Packard entering the front gates and quietly rolling around the circle drive. As the car stops at the front door, a lady emerges, her finger-waved hair bejeweled with Art Deco diamond ornaments. She hears music and laughter from the party inside, and with a few elegant steps disappears into the house.

This California villa was *made* for parties. When we saw it the very first time, even in its rather sad condition, the empty rooms and tired landscaping played the faint music from long-past garden parties. But I also heard something else. As strange as it sounds, I heard the house whisper, "Help me!" How could one resist a call from such a refined damsel in distress? Hopelessly seduced, we made our offer and soon found ourselves the owners of a villa. Or perhaps it was the reverse.

This was a house of dreams, and it certainly fulfilled more than a few of mine. For one, it allowed me to express my passion for Italian style on a grander scale. Plans were drawn up for the renovation, and we soon got to work. The interior was gutted without

ABOVE The restored facade of the Villa delle Favole sports an awning supported by posts surmounted by elaborate finials designed by Matthew White.

RIGHT The old boxwood parterre provides a meandering path to the villa, while recently added garden urns frame the lawn.

remorse, as most of the original detail had been stripped away decades before. I reconfigured and reinvented those details to fulfill my own ideas of what they could have, or perhaps should have, been.

Some rooms were restored to their original configuration, while doorways were realigned and the flow was refined. Anyone who has restored old houses knows that they speak. They give guidance and tell stories. Under no uncertain terms, this house led the way, and I happily followed her sage advice.

We also worked on the garden, and over the years it attained an almost ethereal presence. The ballooning boxwood was drastically cut back, and with persistent hand-clipping, the parterre regained its architectural form. Dying roses were replaced, while old surviving bushes were nourished back to their full glory. In all, we had more than five hundred rose bushes. Long-ignored olive and citrus trees, planted seventy-five years prior, were lovingly pruned and reshaped. Then we added statuary, garden urns, and benches, many of them brought back from Italy. Garden ornament is to the garden what the perfect jewel is to a simple gown: It enhances it and brings focus.

The once-tired garden now glimmered like an old gem, and behind its gates, various celebrations took place. Summer croquet parties, lunch by the pool, dinners in the courtyard, masked balls ... the possibilities for creative entertaining seemed endless. The beauty of the gardens enveloped every guest with a shimmering cloak of verdant green. Anyone who entered the garden walls felt lucky to be there. And indeed, we all were.

Houses contain more than objects; they hold the events of our lives, and this one certainly did for us. Our beloved dog Phoebe died there at a ripe old age, and even today I can still see her, blind and almost entirely white, wandering the garden like a ghost trying to remember her golden youth. We celebrated big birthdays and important anniversaries and welcomed a new puppy into our life. We were fortunate to be able to throw parties small and large, all worthy of the house and that splendid lady in the Packard. ▓

RIGHT Vintage photographs of the boxwood parterre and a tiled fountain give a sense of how the garden looked in the 1920s, but masked balls and other festivities made full use of the mature garden in its more recent splendor. Matthew White and Thomas Schumacher, far right, center, stand in a gondola that floats in the pool for a Venetian-inspired garden party, while "gondoliers" carry sweets in miniature boats. Statuary brought over from Florence creates an elegant connection to the verdant settings of Italy's past and defines an ideal place for contemplation and celebration.

We called this house Villa delle Favole ("House of Myths and Fairytales"). And like a true Italian villa, the surrounding garden was as important as the major rooms, if not more so. Here, villa and garden were linked as one: A magical marriage of inside and out made each space feel perfect in its own right. But truth be told, one would have been vastly diminished without the other. The only room with any original architectural detail was the library—and what a room! To my eye it was perfect, even when empty. It embraced a tiled courtyard to the north, clipped Italian-style parterres to the west, and a rose-filled garden to the east. The old tiled floor and wall of leaded glass fit both the period of the house and

the period that inspired the house, without making either seem less important. It was a romantic, confident room, comfortable in its own skin. On the first day we saw the villa, lost vistas were quietly waiting to be discovered. But we knew that within the walls of the house and its gardens lay the dream of an idealized

life. A charmed atmosphere seemed to surround the villa like a faint, lingering perfume. It was, in a word, magic. In the entry, I designed a new stair railing to replace a fairly recent one that had been clumsily made. I searched for the perfect antique lantern but never found one, so I finally designed my own. Rather than using color, I chose to create a completely neutral foyer that would draw

one into the more colorful rooms. Above the antique hall seat, I created a bracket to hold a marble bust; above the stairs, I hung eighteenth-century angels. For the living room, I replaced a pink, fake–Louis XV mantel with one I had designed in limestone. Instead of a painting or a mirror, I chose to place a large architectural urn above it. Skimpy

moldings were replaced with moldings that had more strength, to reflect the exterior architecture. I created a double sofa, covered it in red Fortuny fabric, and then surrounded it with tapestries and other antiques we had collected over the years. I wanted the room to embrace all who entered it with warm color and vivid history.

The dining room was inspired by a pair of Venetian carved monkeys once owned by the great designer (and my idol) Billy Baldwin. I found them in an auction catalog and recognized them at once from *Billy Baldwin Decorates*, which I had read as a youth. I designed trompe l'oeil frescoes for every wall, to reflect the landscape outside while also suggesting the interior of a garden folly. Instead of a chandelier, I used an overscale garden lantern. Libraries are generally my favorite rooms, and this one was no different. Using leather, limestone, parchment, wood, burnished gold leaf, and antique globes, I created a room without color.

No attempt was made to incorporate the books into the library's decor—these were real books we actually read, not books purchased for their looks. Other than fresh flowers, our books provided the only color in the room. At the top of the stairs, I gutted and redesigned the landing, crowning it with a simple coffered ceiling. This meant taking off the roof and moving it up. Previously this was a low, awkward area that had rather stunted French doors. It had no purpose other than to connect various rooms both upstairs and down. Before the renovation it was an unattractive, glorified space, but afterwards it was transformed into a spot of symmetry and charm. It became a gallery for an ancient Roman torso while providing sweeping views of the garden.

Thanks to the new vertical volume and the elegantly proportioned doors, it flooded the house with light, making it a very important room indeed. The master bedroom, bathroom, and dressing rooms were rendered in quiet colors for a serene, restful setting. I concocted the canopy bed, which was inspired by the baldachins I had seen in Italian churches. I created the fireplace by incorporating an eighteenth-century French panel that gave the hearth a simple, country charm. Like in the dressing room and bathrooms, I designed simple cabinetry for the kitchen and butler's pantry. These highly functional spaces were fashioned to recall the efficient American service rooms of the 1920s.

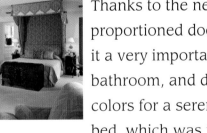

DOSSO DOSSI
Court Painter in Renaissance Ferrara   THE METROPOLITAN MUSEUM OF ART

GRAN TEATRO LA FENICE

PALAZZI OF ROME

Bartolozzi
Montelupo
Villa delle Favole

"Rome was the great object of our pilgrimage ... My temper is not very susceptible of enthusiasm, and the enthusiasm which I do not feel I have ever scorned to affect. But at the distance of twenty-five years I can neither forget nor express the strong emotions which agitated my mind as I first approached and entered the eternal City." —From The Autobiographies of Edward Gibbon, *1796*

During the fourteenth century, the great power of Italy resided in Florence. That strength derived from the fact that Florence was the banking center of Europe. From this power the Renaissance was born, creating the greatest blossoming of art and science in Europe since antiquity. Great palaces were built to house, and protect, Florentine merchant families and their newly acquired wealth.

These palazzi had stone facades more akin to medieval towers when compared to the relative openness of palaces of later ages. The interiors, however, were filled with artistic marvels displayed in magnificently frescoed rooms. As peace became more prevalent, these urban exteriors started to incorporate a lighter feel through classical architectural elements.

OPPOSITE An antique engraving of the Palazzo Farnese illustrates one of Rome's great Renaissance palaces.

Toward the end of the Renaissance, the Medici family's influence weakened and the intellectual and artistic power moved from Florence to Rome. During this period, many great Roman palaces were built, among them the Palazzo Farnese and the Palazzo Spada. The Palazzo Spada was in many ways a traditional Italian Renaissance palace, with a central courtyard and a very solid facade. The ground floor had the effect of rusticated stone, with windows protected by the crossed-iron bars typical for the period. But the upper floors told a different story. There, as if to announce the extravagance of its owner, was a lavish display of swags, garlands, ribbons, and figures, all in detailed stucco relief. Niches were filled with statuary, and portals were surmounted by family crests. These elements signified the Mannerist movement of the late Renaissance. The architect was Bartolomeo Baronino, but

the decoration was in the hands of Giulio Mazzoni. Criticism at the time rejected the sumptuous ornamentation, but this treatment simply foreshadowed the far more exuberant Baroque period still to come.

In the 1630s, the palace was purchased by Cardinal Bernardino Spada and his brother Virgilio. They added a wing and restored some of the interiors while redesigning others in true Baroque taste. A gallery on the second floor was devoted to the cardinal's collection of paintings and sculpture. In the Salone di Pompeo, a statue of someone believed to be Pompey the Great took pride of place. Legend has it that Julius Caesar was murdered at the foot of this statue. Also in the villa is a throne room, which speaks to the importance of the visitors to this house.

The exterior ornamentation of the Palazzo Spada could have been an inspiration to the

American architect Stanford White as he designed the Robb House in New York in the late 1880s. But while the decorative relief on the Palazzo Spada is rendered in stucco and is decidedly more elaborate, White was able to achieve finely detailed ornamentation by using terra-cotta. Although they are separated by an ocean and more than three centuries, both buildings express architectural ideas based on centuries of Italian style. ▣

LEFT The elaborate surface ornamentation of the sixteenth-century facade of the Palazzo Spada in Rome, Italy, was controversial in its time.

THE VILLARD HOUSES

NINETEENTH-CENTURY PALAZZO-STYLE RESIDENCES

The nineteenth century was a period of a multitude of influences on American architecture and decorative arts, some with more credence than others. The endless Victorian style parade included Egyptian Revival, Colonial Revival, Queen Anne, Gothic Revival, Second Empire, and many others. It seemed inevitable that eventually there would be an Italianate style.

The nineteenth-century Italianate villa was not so much created from a study of authentic Italian architecture as it was from a superficial, though charming, Italian affectation. Like many mid-nineteenth-century styles, it was a stylistic effect pasted onto fashionable architectural forms of the period, this time with Romanesque arches and a square tower to define the "style." Edith Wharton refers to one of these American houses in her novel *The Age of Innocence:* "People had always been told that the house at Skuytercliff was an Italian villa. Those who had never been to Italy believed it; so did some who had. The house had been built by Mr. van der Luyden in his youth, on his return from the 'grand tour' ..."

This love of Italian design, even if it was of the Victorian pastiche variety, showed an attraction to the romance Italy held for nineteenth-century Americans. Later in the century, however, a real attraction to, and serious study of, the classical ideals of ancient Rome and the Renaissance began. Architectural historians refer to the period starting in the 1870s as the American Renaissance. This artistic movement, which lasted into the twentieth century, showed an increased interest in European design, especially that of Italy. Students of architecture were required to study books by Vitruvius, Alberti, and Palladio, a curriculum that is sadly lacking in many architectural programs today. It was a time when artists and designers valued the relationship forged by scholarship, science, and art to create a very similar intellectual climate to that of the Italian Renaissance.

One of the finest examples of nineteenth-century domestic architecture inspired by such principles is the structure known as the Villard Houses, built between 1882 and 1885 in New York and designed by the prestigious architectural firm of McKim, Mead, and White. Joseph Wells, a leading architect of the firm, designed the exteriors. This urban residential building included six houses, making it an innovative and supremely elegant version of a multi-family dwelling. Fortunately, this building still exists. Its link to Italy is direct and undeniable.

As an early example of Renaissance Revival architecture, it stands apart.

The sobriety and restraint of the design was revolutionary in New York, and for decades to come it was an important influence on American architecture. At the time it was built, the edifice was considered one of America's most superb domestic structures, not only for the elegant simplicity of the exterior but also for the quality of the interiors. Of the Villard Houses, Stanford White said that it was "the beginning of any good work that we have done ... designed on simple and dignified classic lines, which we have ever since endeavored to follow."

OPPOSITE ABOVE Palazzo Farnese was in its time considered one of the four marvels of Rome. The palace, built between 1515 and 1589, was designed by some of the greatest architects of the age—Antonio da Sangallo the Younger, Michelangelo, Giacomo da Vignola, and, finally, Giacomo delle Porta. Today it remains one of the best examples of an urban Renaissance palazzo. The interiors are lavishly decorated with superb frescoes.

OPPOSITE BELOW The Villard Houses, in New York City—designed by McKim, Mead, and White and completed in 1885—are among the first and perhaps finest example of Renaissance Revival architecture in the United States.

THE ROBB HOUSE

A RENAISSANCE REVIVAL URBAN PALAZZO

In 1889, three brownstones were demolished to make room for a house designed by McKim, Mead, and White. The owners of the soon-to-be-built Renaissance Revival house were James Hampden Robb and his wife, Cornelia Van Rensselaer Robb. Stanford White was the principal architect on the project, and he worked closely with Robb on every detail.

American architects of the 1880s had a deep understanding of the buildings of antiquity and the Renaissance. Joseph Wells—a lead architect at McKim, Mead, and White—said, "The classical ideal suggests clearness, simplicity, grandeur, order, and philosophical calm." That statement is reflected in the design of the Robb House. Apparently, the firm was so enamored of classical Italy and the Renaissance that, in their offices, McKim was called Bramante, and White was referred to as Bellini, after the two great masters.

Once the Robb House was completed, an architecture critic wrote: "The most dignified structure ... not a palace, but a fit dwelling house for a first-rate citizen." In the age of robber barons, this home was by no means over-the-top—not when one considers the near-royal excesses of the age. Yet while this house wasn't deemed a palace in its time, it was by any standard quite grand. The Robb House was three times the size of the average brownstone and had five floors, a magnificent staircase, and vast rooms with period ceilings and monumental fireplaces. In the entrance hall stood a pair of enormous porphyry urns. The walls were enriched by multitudes of superb tapestries, while floors were covered in rare Persian carpets, many dating from the sixteenth century.

The exterior of the Robb House was made of Roman brick with highly detailed terra-cotta ornamentation. Flanking the entrance were double granite columns supporting a two-story porch. The overall shape of the building is a block, massive and somber, much inspired by late-Renaissance palaces and very appropriate

LEFT Three New York City brownstones were torn down to make room for the Robb House, an urban palazzo designed by McKim, Mead, and White in the late 1880s and completed in 1891.

for urban New York. The dining room of the house was paneled in oak and embellished with soaring leaded windows and an elaborate plasterwork-and-oak coffered ceiling. Dominating the space was a massive fireplace designed to hold an enormous sixteenth-century wooden altar. Incorporated throughout the dining room design, both in its carvings and its leaded glass, are oak leaves and acorns. Stanford White referred to this space as the Oak Room.

By 1912, Robb had died and his heirs sold the contents of the house at auction. The sale was held in the grand ballroom of the Plaza Hotel and attended by much of New York society, including Mr. and Mrs. William Rockefeller. Among the many objects sold were an Italian Renaissance relief of the Madonna and child (purchased by the Metropolitan Museum of Art) and a sixteenth-century Persian rug, which went for the then-astronomical sum of $22,000. Also in the sale was the antique Italian painted, coffered ceiling from Robb's private library.

More than a decade later, in 1923, the building was purchased by the Advertising Club, a private organiza-tion that occupied the structure until the 1960s. In 1946,

ABOVE AND RIGHT In the 1920s, the Robb House was turned into the Advertising Club. Possibly the most important antique architectural element in the house, the carved-stone Italian Renaissance fireplace in the sitting room was removed during the building's conversion into apartments in the 1970s.

a fire destroyed some of the rooms on the third floor and above. Miraculously, the facade was untouched and the major rooms of the piano nobile were undamaged. In 1977, the structure was transformed into an apartment building with sixteen units. It was then that many of the important antique architectural elements were torn out. The most valuable piece removed was an Italian Renaissance fireplace from one of the sitting rooms. (Given the tumultuous history of this building, it is a miracle that any of the original interiors have remained remotely intact.)

In 1893, two years after the Robb House was completed, Charles McKim founded the American Academy in Rome. He said: "As Rome went to Greece, and later France, Spain, and other countries had gone to Rome for their own reactions to the splendid standards of Classic and Renaissance Art, so must we become students, and delve, bring back, and adapt to conditions here, a groundwork on which to build."

More than a century later, I was inspired to follow a similar path. By taking inspiration from the past—ancient Rome, Renaissance Italy, and Stanford White's New York—I created a place for living in the twenty-first century. The result is a home steeped in two millennia of Italian history yet created by, and for, Americans. ▣

RIGHT Sidewalk flower shops give bursts of color to New York streets while rushing taxis are noisy reminders that this Stanford White mansion is no longer basking in the Gilded Age. Original leaded-glass windows, a long-lost coffered ceiling, and a recently discovered original mosaic floor all take one back to slower times, when carriages cluttered the avenues. A brochure shows a later use of the Robb House, before it became apartments. Matthew White's living room was photographed as it was in the 1920s, while, more recently, festive evening attire is at the ready.

The former dining room of the Robb mansion is now the living room of our apartment. When I first laid eyes on this room, I fell in love with its proportions and its link to the Gilded Age of New York. But as impressive as the space was, it was in sorry shape. Inappropriate bookcases had been added around the fireplace, while the absence of the sixteenth-century altar that Stanford White had used as the overmantel made the proportions of the fireplace completely wrong. In order to restore the proper proportions to the fireplace, I designed a new overmantel to hold an ancient bust. There was simply no way to authentically replicate the missing antique altar, so reinvention felt like a more appropriate way to complete the most important feature in the room. I also replaced an awkwardly situated and overly large staircase with a more elegant, open set of curving stairs. This allowed for a better flow through the apartment and created a niche for a hall table. The current dining room of the apartment was originally the sitting room next to the Robb Oak Room. When the house was built, it held a superb Italian Renaissance fireplace. When the house was divided into apartments, however, the fireplace was removed and sold, and the grand room was carved into pieces, giving the upper half to the apartment upstairs. That left a new, oddly proportioned dining room with a very low ceiling. Rather than attempt to invent a Stanford White–style space in what was now a low-slung dining room, I chose to create a simple, classical effect that would hold its own without competing with the grand living room. I designed faux-limestone-block walls, with a niche for a seventeenth-century Italian sculpture. This niche takes advantage of hidden space by concealing extra storage for linens and dishes.

I placed an enormous painting from the studio of Giovanni Paolo Pannini at the end of the room to create a view where there had been none. It is fitting that the painting represents the height of grand-tour taste, since my design for the apartment drew its inspiration from Italy during the time when travelers flocked to admire her art and architectural treasures.

In the living room, I linked the wainscot with the coffered ceiling by covering the walls between the two elements in a lush brown Italian damask. This unified the space while giving it richness and texture. Although the brown damask makes the room darker than a lighter fabric would have, it creates a simpler background for the furnishings and works of art. The somberness of the deep brown becomes a perfect foil for the vivid green of the velvet sofas. Upstairs, the

bedroom, bathrooms, and library felt more like a 1970s apartment than spaces in a great Stanford White house. Here again I sought to create a visual link to the living room without trying to compete with the nineteenth-century splendor of its architecture. In the stairwell, I replaced a very 1970s railing with one made of bronze and then hung an iron lantern and created a corbel for an enormous bust of Hercules. I gutted the bathroom and removed a dropped ceiling, which allowed me to take

advantage of the vertical space by adding a barrel-vaulted ceiling. I then tiled the bathroom with a clean, white marble mosaic. The bedroom was originally Robb's private library, which had boasted leaded-glass windows and an antique Italian coffered ceiling, now sadly gone. Faced with a plain box, I added overscale crown moldings. Stylistically, this room takes a departure from Italy, just as the vessels of Venice did when they sailed away to bring back precious cargo from the Orient. The room is

in jewel tones of sapphire and ivory and accented with gold to form a cool counterpoint to the other rooms in the apartment. I designed the domed canopy bed to repeat the silhouette of the antique Indian miniature temple. The bed is trimmed in fringe made by hand from carved bone and vermeil beads, while inside it hangs a nineteenth-century portrait in the Mogul style. Opposite the bed is a large storage cabinet I designed; its mirrored panels suggest

the arched windows of the Near East or Venice. This apartment offers more than a bit of time travel, which I know is not everyone's vision of what a twenty-first-century urban setting should look like. But for me it really works. It combines my personal passion for antiquity and history with a desire to retain a sense of civility in an increasingly uncivilized world. This home not only supplies that civility, it embodies it. 🔲

"The Venetians deserve a special note as the only European people who appear to have sympathized to the full with the great instinct of the Eastern races ... covering their palaces with porphyry and gold." —John Ruskin, The Stones of Venice, 1851

No city in the world is a more alluring melting pot of Eastern and Western styles than Venice. Every arched window and each glittering facade stands as a glamorous testament to the admiration Venetians had for the art and architecture of the Eastern Mediterranean. And yet each architectural element shows how Venice took that style and made it uniquely its own.

Given the republic's mastery of the sea and its unique setting as the only major city on the eastern coast of Italy, it was inevitable that trade with points east would become the prime source of wealth for Venice. The Ottomans of Turkey, the Safavids in Iran, and the Mamluks from Egypt to Syria were but a few of the peoples and places with which the Venetians traded to keep their richly stocked warehouses full. Venice was also the busiest launching

OPPOSITE Although the Palazzo Dario, built in the 1480s, is one of the smaller palaces on Venice's Grand Canal—it is one of the most admired. Its elegant facade has many traditional Italian Renaissance features yet also incorporates rare colored stones and designs inspired by the Middle East.

point from Europe for those making pilgrimages to the Holy Land.

The richness of the Orient made Venetians very rich themselves, creating the perfect climate for opulent display in architecture, interior design, fashion, and the arts. No power in Europe understood luxury, or how to display it, better than Venice in its prime.

Pietro Casola, a Milanese priest who traveled through Venice in 1494 on his pilgrimage to the Holy Land, thought that Milan possessed the most ample assortment of products from around the world—until he saw the Venetian wares. He wrote in his journal: "Who could count the many shops so well furnished that they also seem warehouses, with so many cloths of every make—tapestry, brocades, and hangings of every design, carpets of every sort, camlets of every color and texture, silks of every kind; and so many warehouses full of aromatics, spices, and drugs, and so much beautiful white wax! These things stupefy the beholder and cannot be fully described to those who have not seen them."

Venetian artists, architects, and craftsmen were influenced by these Eastern riches, as well as by the countless stories of the Venetians who had traveled afar to gather them. Persian rugs and textiles appeared in both religious and secular paintings, while Venetian weavers copied Middle Eastern textile patterns in sumptuous silk velvet woven with golden thread. By using these designs for secular purposes, Venetians were showing off their worldly elegance. When the designs were adopted for Christian art, the painter was creating a symbolic connection to the Old Testament. The admiration Venetians had for the artistry of the East permeated all manner of goods, from glass and ceramics to metalwork and bookbinding.

The architecture of Venice also shows a strong connection to the Islamic world. Elegant arched windows, glittering mosaics, rare marbles, and asymmetrical facades are but a few of the elements that display the influence of Islamic culture on Venetian architecture. Giovanni Dario, a well-known diplomat and

LIDO DI VENEZIA - Gondola sul mare dell' Excelsior P

secretary of the Venetian legation to the court of the Ottoman emperor Mehmet II, built his palace in the late fifteenth century, and in doing so, he chose to enhance the facade with exotic references while blending it with more purely Renaissance features. Precious colored marbles, presumably brought back from a diplomatic mission, were used to create a link to similar decorative effects found in the Near East.

This admiration for the exotic had been a part of Venice for so many centuries that it became a sort of vernacular style. The style was deeply informed by Venetian trade and foreign relations and reached its height between 1300 and 1500. Even when the rest of Renaissance Italy became enamored with the classical Western world, Venice, in the main, seemed to prefer her link to points east.

In the late nineteenth and early twentieth centuries, the enthusiasm for Near Eastern styles continued. The grand Hotel Excelsior, on the Lido in Venice, was built in 1908 to attract wealthy travelers to the beaches of the Adriatic. With its Turkish-style arches and ballooning domes, the hotel is an early-twentieth-century example of how Venice once again turned to the Eastern Mediterranean for inspiration.

In the decorative arts, Mariano Fortuny created hanging lamps influenced by Eastern pendants and printed textiles with designs directly inspired by the Islamic world. As a collector of Oriental and Near Eastern artifacts, and as an artist living in a Venetian Gothic palazzo, Fortuny exemplified how one could easily fall under the spell of these styles. In his unique way, Fortuny carried on a centuries-old tradition, just as many Venetian merchants, artists, and craftsmen had before him.

The influence of the Islamic world on design in Venice has a long, fascinating history. Whether depicted on bookbindings or marble facades, Venice used these designs to show the world its power and share her love of beauty. The result was a European capital like no other. Even without the canals, which render Venice an utterly unique setting for urban life, these distant influences make "La Serenissima" a place of visual mystery and otherworldly exoticism. ▩

LEFT The early-twentieth-century Hotel Excelsior, on the Lido in Venice, is depicted in a vintage postcard. With its Turkish-style windows and overall exotic appearance, the building continues a long tradition in Venice of looking to the Near East for artistic inspiration.

CENTRAL SYNAGOGUE, NEW YORK
OLANA, ON THE HUDSON

Architecture inspired by the Islamic world was fairly rare in nineteenth-century America, but it did exist. In the later part of the century, Orientalist art became a movement and spawned an atmosphere of increased interest in the exotic. This style filtered to America through a variety of sources, with Venice and Andalusia, Spain, being the primary European links.

American Orientalist buildings were most often created for commercial or religious use. Many were places of entertainment, such as theaters, opera houses, hotels, or stores that sold exotic wares. These seemed appropriate uses for what most Americans regarded as a highly theatrical style. Many of the best surviving American examples of this style, however, are synagogues.

Because of the centuries of persecution in Europe, Jews had not been able to develop an architectural style in the West that was uniquely their own. With the emancipation of Jews in Europe during the nineteenth and early twentieth centuries and the rapid growth of the Jewish population in both Europe and America, there came an opportunity, and a need, for an architectural style to define their places of worship. The classical style of Greece was perhaps considered too pagan; that of Rome, perhaps too Catholic; and the Gothic style had for centuries been linked to Christianity.

Given that Jerusalem was in the Middle East, it seemed logical to create a revival style based on ideas from that part of the world. The first major synagogue in the Moorish Revival style was built in the 1830s in Munich. From then on in Europe, and later in America, this style would be the most typical choice for Jewish houses of worship.

In 1870, construction began on New York's Central Synagogue, which was designed by the German-trained architect Henry Fernbach, who may have seen its Munich predecessor. Central Synagogue, the oldest synagogue in continual usage in New York, is a superb representation of the nineteenth-century Moorish, or Arabic, Revival style.

Domestic structures in this style are rarer. One notable example is Olana, the home of the

American landscape painter Frederic Edwin Church. This house, with its spectacular view of the Hudson River, was built in the early 1870s.

In 1867, Church bought the hilltop overlooking a farm he had owned for a number of years. It had been his dream to build a house on that hill, and when he finally acquired it, he hired Richard Morris Hunt to design the house. Although some elements of Hunt's design were incorporated into Olana, the overall scheme was not to Church's liking. After a trip with his wife and young son to Europe, the Middle East, and North Africa, Church came back to New York with renewed inspiration for his exotic villa.

He then hired Calvert Vaux, an architect who would be more open to Church's strong ideas and be far more flexible and collaborative than Hunt, who apparently had no interest in playing second fiddle to Church's firm views. When the house was completed, Church stated: "I designed the house myself. It is Persian in style adapted to the climate and requirements of modern life. The interior decorations and fittings are all in harmony with the external architecture."

Certainly the artist had a vision, not only for the house but also for the property. After dredging a large lake from marshland and planting trees to create an ideal view, he said, "I can make more and better landscapes in this way than by tampering with canvas and paint in the studio."

Like the Venetian palazzo, built to reflect an interest in the art and architecture of the Near East, these American examples also make use of polychrome effects on the exteriors. The rich facades are an essential part of the style and a contrast to the more sober materials of the classical Western model. Arched windows, pointed or rounded, also create an immediate link to Persia and Turkey, as compared to Giovanni Dario's choice of a more Italian-style arched fenestration on his Venetian palazzo. The long history of Islamic culture's influence on design in the West may have had its early expression in Venice, but the allure of this aesthetic didn't stop there. During the American Century, hundreds of years after the golden age of Venetian architecture, this fascination with the East found its place in the New World. ▩

OPPOSITE Central Synagogue in New York City, built in the 1870s, remains one of the finest examples of Moorish architecture in the United States.

RIGHT Olana, designed by the American landscape painter Frederic Edwin Church, was built in upstate New York in the 1870s, after the artist's long tour through Europe, the Middle East, and North Africa. His unique vision created this magical, Persian-inspired villa that also recalls Venetian palaces.

CASTLE GREEN

A PENTHOUSE LOFT INSPIRED BY VENICE AND THE NEAR EAST

In the mid-nineteenth century, the fertile soil and abundant water of California's San Gabriel Valley drew settlers who planted orchards and, ultimately, orange groves. As the small population proliferated, others were drawn by the area's healthful climate and agricultural opportunity. New railways would open the territory to travelers, many from New England and eager to escape dreary, cold winters. The proud founders of Pasadena worked hard to enhance the already prodigious charms of their growing city.

Eventually, small inns were replaced with enormous hotels that provided every possible comfort. One of the most famous was the Hotel Green. An early brochure for the hotel described Southern California's charms: "Chief among its garden spots is the far-famed San Gabriel Valley, cradling in its lap the lovely city of Pasadena, with its ideal homes, its beautiful orange groves, and its wilderness of gorgeous flowers. Becoming a mecca of the tourist, it soon demanded accommodation for the visitor in keeping with its environment."

The spectacular Hotel Green redefined luxury in a place where, in the eighteenth century, there had been only the San Gabriel Mission, a few rancheros, and the Gabrielino Indian tribe. In the mid-nineteenth century, Pasadena was a small farming community. By the end of the nineteenth century, Pasadena was the third-largest city in California and a destination resort. Picturesquely nestled beneath the San Gabriel Mountains, this bustling town was dubbed Crown of the Valley.

The Hotel Green complex comprised three large buildings and covered two city blocks. Designed by architect Frederick L. Roehrig, the buildings were constructed over a period of years and linked together with an unusual enclosed bridge spanning Raymond Street. Beneath this bridge, the street thronged with pedestrians, elegant carriages, bicycles, cable cars, and the

new automobile. The Hotel Green was unique in that it had its own stop on the Santa Fe railway line, before the train pulled in to the Pasadena station. This allowed the hotel's well-heeled patrons to be whisked up to their rooms immediately, while porters and maids followed behind with steamer trunks and hatboxes.

Castle Green, completed in 1899, was the second building to go up in the hotel complex. As one of the first steel-frame structures in California, it was widely advertised to be fireproof—an important feature when one considers that the 200-room Raymond Hotel spectacularly went up in flames in 1895.

Architecturally, Castle Green had many influences, and key among them was the exoticism of the East: Windows were shaped with Moorish arches and delicate tracery, balconies and loggias added romance, and two domes crowned the imposing edifice. In fact, the Lido's Hotel Excelsior was built eight years after Castle Green and, with its domes and Moorish windows, is strikingly similar to the American hotel. Castle Green's unique style stood apart in nineteenth-century Pasadena— and still turns heads today.

In its heyday, the Hotel Green's vine-draped loggias and rooftop gardens drew an affluent, influential group of guests, including presidents, movie stars, and crowned heads of Europe. It was the center of social life in a town that attracted millionaires from cold climes, many arriving in private train cars. Some of these wealthy families, such as the Wrigleys and the Gambles, decided to stay in Pasadena after their first visit. They built palatial winter homes and established sprawling, elaborate gardens that soon led to Pasadena's being called the Rose City.

A vintage brochure touted the attributes of the Hotel Green: "The architecture of the buildings permits many surprises in the way of cozy corners and pleasant promenades, away from the busy life of the hotel, where one may rest and dream, drinking in the ... beauties of this Italy in America." One of these cozy corners, located on the top floor, was a large glass-roofed solarium flanked by two expansive roof terraces. The solarium was a palm-filled sanctuary, the perfect place for guests to read the morning paper or take afternoon tea. The roof gardens and balconies offered uninterrupted views of the San Gabriel Mountains, a valley carpeted with fragrant groves and gardens, and, on the western horizon, the glistening Pacific Ocean. It was an Arcadian setting at the start of the American Century.

Pasadena continued to grow, but the resort

RIGHT Originally built as a solarium garden, the glass-topped room of the old Castle Green hotel, in a photograph taken around 1900, was flanked by two outside terraces overlooking bustling Pasadena, orange groves, and the San Gabriel mountains nearby.

"Knowest thou the land where the citron and olive is fairest of fruit, and the voice of the meadowlark never is mute? It is Pasadena." —Thomas Balch Elliott, 1876

era ended with the stock market crash of 1929. Castle Green, no longer a viable business, was purchased by a group of devoted residents who refused to leave their adopted home. Miraculously, the building has survived, a romantic reminder of nineteenth-century travel and the grand style in which it was practiced.

It is difficult to overestimate the allure of Pasadena to early visitors. Today, the Tournament of Roses Parade is a reminder of those halcyon days. In 1890, the parade began its tradition of horse-pulled carriages festooned in mounds of locally grown roses. Professor Charles Holder, a member of the Valley Hunt Club, the organization that inaugurated the parade, said: "In New York, people are buried in snow, here our flowers are blooming and our oranges are about to bear. Let's hold a festival to tell the world about our paradise."

In the 1930s, the solarium of Castle Green was turned into an apartment, just as the other hotel rooms had been. But because the solarium was not designed to be a living space, many modifications were made to create a more habitable layout. Its arched colonnade was walled in to create a separate bedroom, bath, kitchen, and dining room, while the original steel trusses were encased in clumsy wooden beams. The glass ceiling was covered to minimize heat intake during summer months.

As the country's economy faltered, the building became a crumbing reminder of better days and was inhabited by eccentrics who had enjoyed the hotel in its prime. Today it is part of the rejuvenated Old Town of Pasadena and benefits from great efforts of historic preservation. It is now a National Historic Landmark and remains one of Pasadena's most singular architectural treasures. 🏛

RIGHT Nestled in a valley of orange groves at the turn of the twentieth century, the Hotel Green took pride of place in Pasadena. Vintage postcards show its instant romance and architectural exoticism. Blending Eastern and Western styles, Matthew White conjured a penthouse and roof garden inspired by both Venice and the building itself. With candles blazing and windows thrown open to take in soft California breezes, this unique space was the ideal spot for entertaining and viewing the panoramic vistas.

After we sold the Villa delle Favole and moved to New York, we searched for a California pied-à-terre. I had just completed the design of a client's apartment at Castle Green and through this relationship learned that the penthouse would soon be available. When I saw it, the space was much as it had been in the 1930s. I then saw photographs of the room as a solarium circa 1900, and the desire to restore it became overwhelming. We signed the lease—and took on a historic preservation project in the bargain. By restoring the arches, we opened up the walled-in bedroom and dining room, and in doing so, we simultaneously returned the solarium to its historic configuration and created the ultimate twenty-first-century loft. While this nineteenth-century interior might not have suited traditional living situations in the 1930s, the open plan offers the perfect living space for contemporary city life. Putting together the furniture plan, however, was a bit of a challenge. How

does one furnish a room that measures forty feet square and make it feel inviting? I started by dividing the expansive space into areas defined by use. On one side, I planned a large sitting area with a gilded Italian center table as its hub. For the other side, I made an office-library and designed a glass-topped work table that could double as a dinner table for large parties. In the center of the

ample room, I placed a life-size bronze garden figure that we had found in Florence and used in our garden at the villa. This was my nod to the penthouse's original function as an indoor garden. I put an intimate dining area behind the arches and placed the bed in a corner. Because the bedroom had no walls, I swathed the entire area in curtains made from Indian silk. A major design challenge in the penthouse was its lack of closets—there was not a single one in sight, and the interior's historic status prohibited us from installing any. To make the space workable, I designed multiple ways to hide

clothes and necessities without employing standard storage solutions. Although the platform bed and various other pieces of furniture were designed to hold linens and clothing, the lion's share of our effects were stored in a two-story closet made from a steel frame that I had covered in canvas. We accessed the top level of the huge closet with an enormous warehouse-type rolling

staircase that reminded me of the wooden rolling stairs in Fortuny's studio in Venice. For the entrance to the main room, I designed a freestanding partition with closets on one side; this would allow for a more defined foyer and act as a visual buffer, preventing the entire loft from being viewed from the front door. The roof garden came with its own set of challenges: The 2,500-square-foot space was dotted with chimneys that felt randomly placed. I brought order to the chaos by

forming a long allée of inexpensive iron arches purchased from a gardening catalog. These were wired together to create an arbor, which would bring a bit of shade to the sun-blasted roof. Off this central path, I carved out "rooms"—a sitting room here, a dining room there—and outside the apartment's kitchen windows, I installed an outdoor kitchen. As soon as plants were brought up, butterflies and birds followed. Suddenly, we had a garden in the sky. The towering

palm trees that surrounded the building were at eye level, and all around were views of my favorite Pasadena buildings. Sitting in the shade of an umbrella, we could hear mourning doves coo and watch hummingbirds dart from blossom to blossom. Sunrises and sunsets filled the open views to the east and west, and on the Fourth of July we could see firework displays from the Rose Bowl, in Pasadena, to Santa Monica. To me, the entire feel of the penthouse suggests Venice at the turn of the

twentieth century. Of course, there are other elements of Italy that I sprinkled about the place: grand-tour souvenirs, a Venetian gilt-wood chair, and a splendid neoclassical Italian table. A focal point of the space was the enormous convex mirror made entirely out of buttons by the artist Clare Graham; I commissioned the mirror specifically for this room. In spite of our numerous antiques, the loft remains fresh and full of surprises. The very nature of the penthouse exudes a modern sensibility, from the

exposed nineteenth-century iron trusses to the endless light pouring in from every side. It's a timeless space, not wedded to any particular period. The apartment incorporates restored and protected historic architecture, a collection of Italian art and objects, and plenty of modern comforts. Although it's steeped in history, it is above all a place for twenty-first-century living. ▣

"Then I climbed a steep and winding way ... to a villa on a hilltop, where I found various things that touched me with almost too fine a point. Seeing them again, often for a week, both by sunlight and moonshine, I never learned not to covet them; not to feel that not being a part of them was somehow to miss an exquisite chance." —Henry James, "Italy Revisited," 1878

The most influential architect in the Western world is Andrea Palladio. His villas, churches, and public buildings remain superb examples of the classical ideal as seen through Renaissance eyes. While these buildings are grand, Palladio's personal origins were not. Born in Padua in 1508, Palladio became an apprentice to a stonemason as a young boy. His father was a miller. While still in his teens, Palladio took a position in Vicenza, working on the houses of the great patrician families of the region.

Because of his obvious talent and learning—as well as his eventual introduction to the nobility in the Veneto and, ultimately, Venice—Palladio rose to fame. His work is now so well known and so often referenced that one can conjure a specific image from the mere mention of his name.

OPPOSITE An antique engraving of Andrea Palladio's La Rotunda shows a higher dome than the one that was ultimately built.

With his perfect sense of scale, light, and space and his informed use of classical ideas, Palladio created houses not of ostentatious style but with noble presence. Unlike the fortresslike feeling of earlier Renaissance villas, Palladio's houses have an openness that celebrates their relationship with the land.

But he did not create these great buildings in a vacuum. He was, after all, an Italian living during one of the most creative periods in Western history—the High Renaissance. He had the great buildings of Venice and Rome to inspire him, though it was clearly the latter city that had the most profound impact on the young architect.

One of these buildings was the Pantheon in Rome. Built during the reign of Emperor Hadrian (A.D. 76–138), and perhaps even designed by Hadrian himself, it remains the largest surviving dome from antiquity made

entirely of unreinforced concrete. How it was built was a question for every architect during the Renaissance and is one that has not been fully answered today. This engineering marvel brought architects from all over Italy and beyond to solve the puzzle. But while no one could fully explain the ancient building techniques used to construct the dome, all, including Palladio, were amazed by the sheer splendor of the place.

La Rotunda, or the Villa Capra, is perhaps Palladio's most famous building and the one most closely linked to the Pantheon. It was built just outside of the town of Vicenza in the late 1560s. And though it is called a villa, it really isn't one at all. Instead, La Rotunda was built for a retired monsignor who apparently used it for parties.

Today the villa enraptures visitors with a sense of magic, just as it did when it was first built. One is drawn to its symmetry and perfect

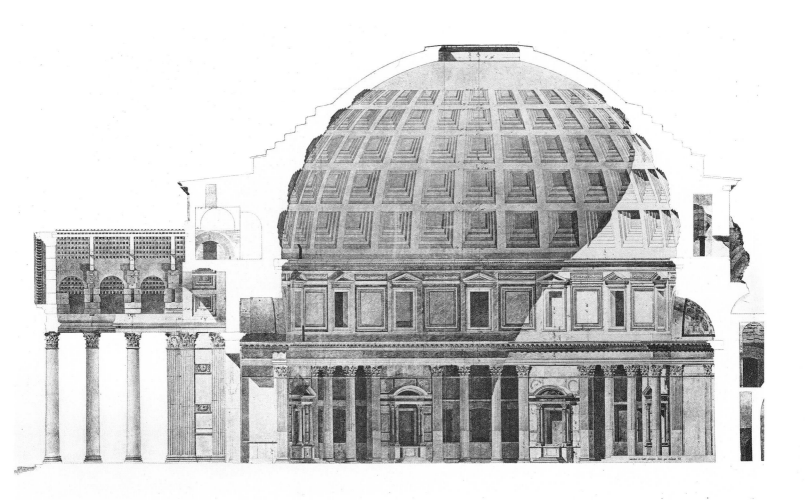

sighting. As soon as one views it from a distance, all else falls away. La Rotunda *beckons*.

Palladio's buildings have been greatly admired for centuries throughout Europe and beyond. Where would the English country house be without Palladio? One can only imagine that it would have remained in the form of forbidding stone castles, Gothic spires, or half-timbered picturesque facades. Without diminishing the superb examples of those styles, Palladio and his classical inspirations were largely responsible for pulling England—and most of Europe—out of the dark ages and into the glorious light. Of course, saying one likes La Rotunda is a bit like saying one likes a cool breeze on a hot day, but never mind. It just feels so right. That's the key. Palladio created places that seem *inevitable*. His villas are never boring or expected—instead, they delight the mind, the eye, and the heart. ▨

OPPOSITE AND ABOVE The Pantheon was built by the Roman emperor Hadrian around A.D. 120 and remains the largest dome surviving from antiquity. It has inspired many major architects through the ages, including Palladio.

"The Pantheon therefore is not only one of the most famous buildings of the ancient world, an iconic touchstone for architects ever since, but it also provides the most authentic glimpse of a purpose-built environment in which Hadrian acted on a public stage." —Thorsten Opper, Hadrian: Empire & Conflict, *2008*

CLASSICAL SPLENDOR

THOMAS JEFFERSON'S MONTICELLO

"I am as happy nowhere else and in no other society, and all my wishes end, when I hope my days will end, at Monticello."

—*Thomas Jefferson, 1787*

In the eighteenth century, the grand tour was at its height. Well-heeled British travelers flooded Italy and came away with art and ideas for their imposing houses back home. Palladio was a major influence who forever changed the idea of what an English country house could be.

Americans were also influenced by Italy, but not all of them actually made the trip. Thomas Jefferson was one of those people. One of America's great "villas," and one of its earliest, is Monticello ("Little Mountain"), the home Jefferson designed for himself in Charlottesville, Virginia. The elegant symmetry of the building, the dome, the classical layout—all directly hark back to Palladio's La Rotunda.

Unlike many of his contemporaries, Jefferson had an extreme distaste for English architecture. As a young man, he had acquired a copy of Giacomo Leoni's translation of Palladio's *Four Books of Architecture,* and in 1769, when Jefferson began building his house, he incorporated Palladio's principles into its design. The process of creating Monticello was a long one, and over the many years it took to build it, Jefferson would tear things out and make improvements along the way. He was constantly experimenting and refining his vision.

In 1785, three years after his wife died, Jefferson was sent to France to serve as a foreign minister. While there, he continued his study of architecture. The French of the eighteenth century were utterly enamored by Italian architecture, and through the study of books such as *Les édifices antiques de Rome* by Antoine Desgodetz, Jefferson gained a clearer focus on how to complete his beloved Monticello. Although he wanted to travel to Italy to see firsthand the places of his passion, he was never able to make the trip. When he returned to America in 1789, he embarked on a dramatic remodeling of Monticello, ultimately creating the house we know today. Construction was completed in 1809, ending forty years of perfecting his American villa.

Monticello was unique in eighteenth-century America in that it looked back to the great buildings of Palladio and ancient Rome yet seemed very contemporary. And because of Jefferson's ingenuity, the house incorporated some original and truly American ideas. The concept of referring to the romance of European history while living in the present and casting an eye toward the future is a completely American trait.

While it can be argued that Jefferson was influenced primarily by French *taste,* the French enthusiasm for Italian *style* is what made Monticello an American villa, not a chateau. ▓

ABOVE LEFT Palladio's La Rotunda (also known as the Villa Capra) is perfectly situated on a gentle hill in the Veneto region of Italy. Crowned by a dome, the structure features an identical temple front on each side. The villa remains one of the most iconic of all the great buildings by the celebrated architect.

LEFT Monticello was based on Jefferson's study of the great buildings of ancient Rome and the Renaissance, especially the those designed by Palladio. Unlike his Early American peers, the third president of the United States was no fan of English architecture and looked instead to Italy for inspiration.

A MODERN HOUSE WITH
ANCIENT ROOTS

We sold our beloved Villa delle Favole, in California, with the idea that we might one day build a country house in the Hudson Valley. Our vision for this new house would be different from what most people look for in a bucolic retreat. We didn't dream of a cabin with a stone fireplace or of a farmhouse filled with folk art, nor did we want a picturesque barn refitted for modern living. Those are all wonderful notions, but they aren't right for us. Our dream was to build a country villa inspired by Rome and Palladio—a place that would recall the ancient houses of Italy but be constructed with an eye for conservation and life today.

While the styles of country houses may vary, rural pleasures remain the same. We were eager to take walks through the woods and sit at a breakfast table laden with hearty food. Bird-watching, shopping at the local farmers' market, and throwing logs on a roaring fire were all part of the dream. We pictured ourselves sharing long dinners with friends, viewing sunsets from the terrace, and napping with a book (and a dog) on our laps. We even hoped to do some organic farming. These activities, and the place and time to enjoy them, are to us the ultimate luxury.

Everyone fantasizes of one day building his or her own dream house; it's an American obsession. Like many people, I dreamed of my ultimate house long before the reality of it was remotely possible. Based on our experience with previous homes, I had very specific ideas about the kinds of rooms we wanted and how we would use them. We had our collections of books, art, and furniture, and I knew that the perfect house for us would be built around this evidence of our history together. All houses are a kind of self-portrait, and we would create ours.

While these dreams were brewing, I tried to keep them in check. I couldn't have them bubble over—at least not until we found a plot of land. During our fantasizing phase, dear friends started to build a house of their own. They found a piece of land in Spencertown, New York, and one day we went out to see the place. We were besotted. "You can actually buy land this beautiful?" we heard ourselves asking. Their house was sited on a gentle hill, backed by a forest and facing the loveliest Hudson Valley view. It was perfection.

Key to the success of their house was the architect Dennis Wedlick. He had created the perfect house for *them,* based on the classic American saltbox but designed in a way that felt completely original. It captured the essence of our friends, their sensibility,

and their passions. We were intrigued.

It wasn't long before we contacted a local agent and our big adventure began. We traipsed through tick-infested thickets, over barren windswept hilltops, and across flat farmland, none of which offered what we were hoping for. We finally came to a property on a quiet country lane. We got out of the car and walked along a stream and up a wooded hill. The entirely undeveloped land and terrain reminded us of Italy. Not ones to waste time, we made an offer, and before we knew it, the land was ours.

Then came the sleepless nights. I always lose sleep when I'm excited about a project and, *boy,* was I ever excited. We had lived in and restored many old houses—and loved every single one. But this was a whole different ball of wax. It is one thing to react to existing architecture, and quite another to make one's own mark on the landscape and create a new vision out of whole cloth. And so there I lay, eyes wide open at three in the morning, inventing apparitions in the dark, images of a place that did not yet exist. I pictured the front gate. I visualized the mystery and delight of motoring up a winding drive through hidden woods to arrive, suddenly, at an enchanted villa. My favorite dreams are the ones that come true.

When I envisioned this phantom villa, I could see much of it with great clarity: The rooms were generous, with elegant, old-fashioned proportions. Windows were placed to look out at Arcadian vistas. I pictured symmetry and order, a house that was classical and calm but also visually exciting, even theatrical. We had experienced all these elements in the many country villas we had visited in Italy. What I couldn't visualize was the exterior. I had no desire to have the outside of the house look like a replica of anything. Villa delle Favole was a true revival style, and as a copy of a Tuscan villa, it had undeniable charm. But this new house had to be something … *other*. I wanted it to suggest Italy, but in a fresh and less literal way.

I reached out to Dennis in an e-mail with my ideas. In my note I said we weren't interested in the typical style of house we saw in our region. I didn't want anything in an Early American style. Colonial houses are beautiful, but they weren't right for us. Much of Dennis' work seemed to cull elements from eighteenth- and nineteenth-century American architecture, yet with each project he devised something new. That was the key. His houses were never bland reissues of a historic style, and I sensed that he could take my ideas and help us create the twenty-first-century villa that we dreamed

OPPOSITE A cross-sectional rendering of Otium shows the domed, double-height living room centered under the rotunda. The villa blends Italian architectural proportions with twenty-first-century green systems such as geothermal heating and solar panels.

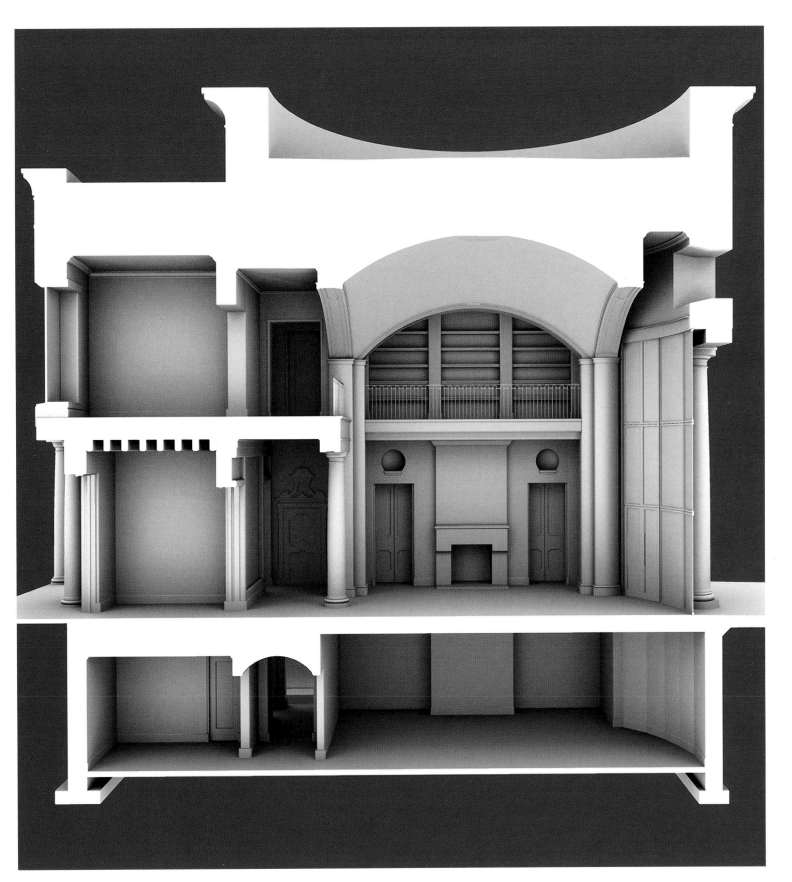

of—a modern house with ancient roots.

Most people select an architect or designer based on a portfolio of past work. They see photographs or renderings of projects and hire a person or firm because they want something similar, if not exactly the same. I had not seen the kind of house I wanted anywhere. It certainly didn't exist in Dennis' portfolio. Yet I loved his *sensibility,* his way of playing with historic precedent with an educated eye and a deft hand. Most of all, I admired the wit in his work. As a designer, I am always surprised when clients ask for something they've seen before. What is the fun in that? No exploration, no excitement— just one more house in a fill-in-the-blank style. Could anything be more deadly dull?

Even though I didn't know Dennis personally, I knew he would appreciate where I was coming from. What creative person wouldn't? He responded favorably to my e-mail, and we set up a meeting. I expressed my thoughts, and Dennis was terrific—open, positive, and very collaborative. He understood how important it was for me to be central to the design of the house and that the process would start from the inside out. He said the perfect thing: "Start designing the floor plan, and we'll refine it together. Once we have something you love, we'll throw sculptures over it and come up with an exterior shape that sings." And that's exactly what we did.

Meanwhile, Dennis visited the property several times. He found a site for the house that was quite different from what we had originally envisioned. We met him there on a warm but overcast spring day, and with our dachshund, Holden, bounding through the woods beside us, we passed the original spot, huffing and puffing, and followed Dennis farther up the hill. Finally, we found ourselves on a sort of platform, like an old meadow now wooded. The trees there were completely different than the surrounding ones. Suddenly, the sun burst out and the brilliant green canopy glowed. At that moment, Dennis announced, "*This* is the magic spot." And was he ever right.

Every time we revisited the site, something mystical happened. A spectacular bird would appear and stay with us, or it would rain everywhere except for where we stood. Once, the wind blew all around us, though our "sweet spot" remained blissfully calm.

RIGHT Otium, in upstate New York, is a house whose design is based on classical and Renaissance ideas. Even though it doesn't repeat the Pantheon's dome, the house has a rotunda. In place of a temple front so loved by Palladio, a curving wall supported by classical columns announces the front entrance.

Dennis had discovered a truly special place.

While we worked out the floor plan, Dennis played with the exterior. He showed us various designs, and they were surprisingly theatrical and very bold. We selected our favorite, one that recalled Palladio's work while in no way repeating the typical references. Although there was no pediment or Palladian windows, the rotunda and the symmetry definitely made the house feel like a modern version of the Palladian ideal. Instead of a pediment over the entrance, there was an embracing curved wall that reminded me of elements we had seen at Hadrian's villa in Tivoli. Our villa's effect was imposing yet human-scaled. It expressed a classical austerity and, at the same time, an exuberance. The house was like nothing we had seen before, but it resonated with us.

From the beginning, I wanted the house to be made of stone and have steel-framed windows. When driving through the Hudson Valley, the stone houses are the ones that always speak to me. I love their sense of solidity and permanence. Plus, a house with low-maintenance exterior finishes appealed to us from a practical standpoint. We had discussed thin Roman brick and even fabricated sample walls, but in the end stone won out. The steel-framed windows, like the stone, were a lower-maintenance, longer-lasting material than wood.

Various green systems were integrated into the house's design: Geothermal power would cool and heat the home, and solar panels on the rotunda's roof would heat the household water. A subterranean cistern in the garden would gather rainwater to irrigate the lawn.

Finally, construction began, and as our "villa on the hill" took shape, so did the rooms, both in my mind and in reality. My workshops were buzzing as they created the lighting and furniture I had designed. As we got closer to completion, soft goods like curtains and bedcovers were made. And then—at last—the day had come. The trucks arrived from California, and the pieces from Villa delle Favole that had been crated and stored for nearly four years finally saw the light of day again. Unwrapping each item was like seeing an old friend. We revived them from a long slumber and welcomed them into their new home—*Otium*. 🦎

RIGHT Ideally situated on a hill, like many romantic villas in Italy, Otium is the vision of Italian style transported to America in the twenty-first century. The seasons provide an endless visual display and appropriate activities, including snowshoeing in winter and bicycling in summer. The most common activity, however, lies in the translation of the house's name, Otium—"leisure informed by art and intellectual pursuits."

I had a very specific idea of the feel I wanted for the rooms at Otium. Heavy plaster walls, minimal door and window casings, and reclaimed-wood flooring were all part of that vision. I hoped that these relatively plain backgrounds and finishes would declare the solidity and monumentality of the exterior while still expressing an unpretentious feel. Even though this was a new house, the feeling I

sought was one that was timeless and true. Given the various colors of the forest, from verdant greens to reds and golds, I decided to keep the rooms fairly neutral. Any color in the living room itself comes from our tapestries, paintings, and antiques. I covered the new pieces of furniture in simple linen and used dark sisal on the floor. On the eighteenth-century Venetian

gilt-wood chair, I replaced red velvet upholstery with pale pony skin. I designed an enormous central lantern with hand-wrought iron laurel branches to crown the main room. At each end of the first-floor gallery, which opens onto the living room, are eighteenth-century Venetian walnut doors. As soon as I saw these, I knew they would be perfect for Otium, so we configured the space to fit them. The garden room was

planned as a sort of screened-in porch. When the doors are thrown open, the sounds of birdsong and the nearby stream come together in the most perfect music. I designed the niche to hold a nineteenth-century plaster cast of the Capitoline Antinous, a sculpture whose original residence is believed to have been at Hadrian's villa, a place

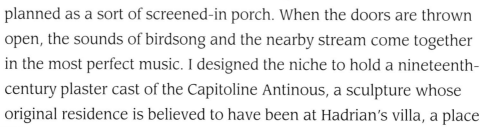

that, along with La Rotunda, provided great inspiration for Otium. The wicker sofa and neoclassical chairs combine to create a multipurpose space where we have breakfast, read, nap, and enjoy the company of weekend guests. Located on the opposite side of the living room from the garden room is the dining room. Its walls are papered in Baroque designs

that I had digitally enlarged from a set of seventeenth-century engravings created by an Italian artist for a French house. On the ceiling, I used an old engraving of an Italian ceiling painting. This modern, monochromatic treatment employs a highly graphic effect to show off an antique design. Flanking a door are a pair of parcel-gilt console

tables with Italian marble urns. Otium has four bedrooms; each of the guest rooms is named after a city on the grand tour—Venice, Rome, and Florence. These rooms are furnished with simple fabrics, mostly cotton and linen, and contain elements that relate to their namesakes. In the

Venetian room, I reused the old Fortuny fabric from the sofa in the Villa delle Favole's living room. On each side of the bed is one of a pair of Venetian wall lanterns held by life-size carved hands. Shades of ivory envelop the master bath and dressing room, and both spaces are decorated with antique busts. For the dressing room, I created a pair of niches above a stack of

drawers to hold a pair of early-nineteenth-century busts of two young brothers. Set on a pedestal behind the tub in the bathroom is a marble bust of the emperor Augustus sporting a necklace created by the great California designer Tony Duquette. Overlooking the living room is a double library

gallery, with two walls lined with bookshelves, and a reading room. In the reading room is a center table formerly owned by Rudolf Nureyev, while at each end of the library galleries are two Venetian monkeys that once belonged to Billy Baldwin. These legends of dance and design represent the major creative influences of my life. The reading room enjoys heart-stopping views of treetops, a faraway

farm, and, in the evening, the setting sun. I designed the two sofas to repeat the gentle curve of the ceiling and created custom-printed fabric with the words *otium litteratum,* which means "leisure spent by reading and writing." Like the great villas of Italy, the garden is a key part of Otium's beauty. But rather than planting elaborate gardens (and fighting

the deer who long to eat them), we embraced our woodland environment, with simple lawns and minimal plantings as our preference. In the spring, thousands of daffodils (*not* the deer's preference) line the long drive up the hill. And we have some lilac bushes, of course. These are all nods to my early days of seeking beauty at the trailer park in Texas—and they still bring much joy.

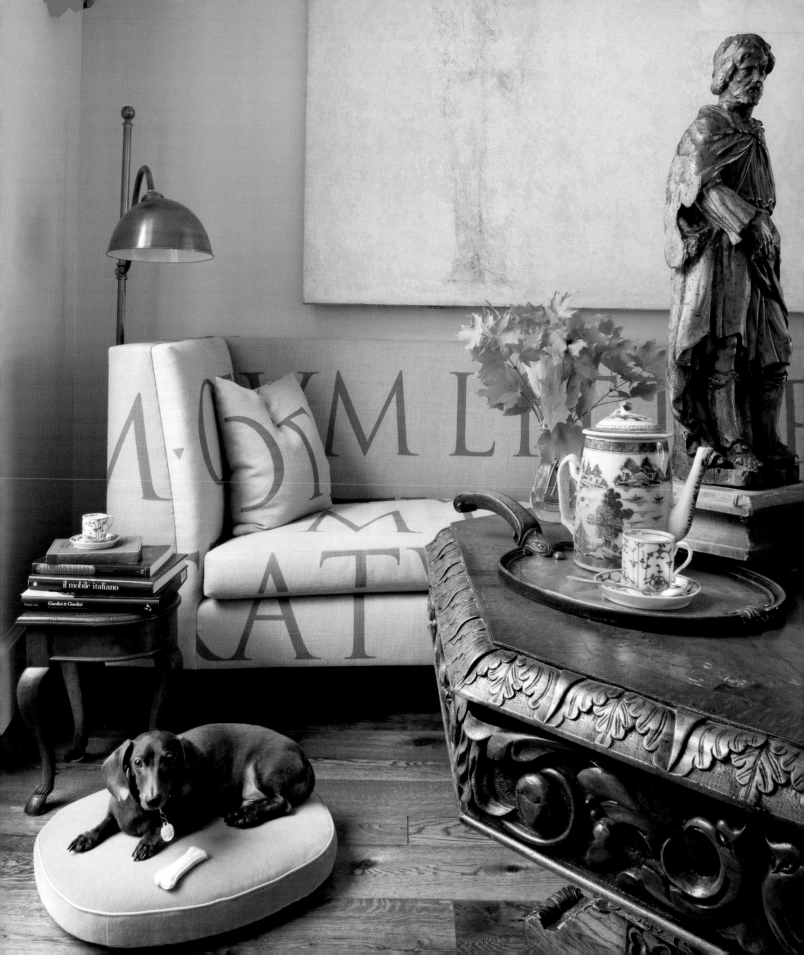

ITALIAN PARKS AND GARDENS

PILOGUE

WHITE WEBB: TECHNOLOGY APPLIED TO
CREATE PURE FANTASY INSPIRED BY ANTIQUITY

"History is the witness that testifies to the passing of time, it illuminates reality, vitalizes memory, provides guidance in daily life, and brings us good tidings of antiquity." —Cicero, First Century B.C.

The twenty-first-century designer is inspired by what is around him. He is therefore inevitably inspired by *the past*. That is as it always has been and how it will be going forward. Those who ignore this fact, or who pretend to ignore it, are fooling themselves. No one designs in a vacuum.

"Past versus present" is a big topic in our design offices at White Webb. My business partner, Frank Webb, is a modernist; I (as anyone can clearly see) am not. This makes for some spirited debates around the project table. When Frank's creative juices get flowing, it is generally because of inspiration of the more recent past. But whether we look back to the great masters of twentieth-century design or cast our glance to ancient Rome, the Etruscans, and beyond, it is still the past. That doesn't stop Frank from teasing me (relentlessly) for being a fusty classicist, or my badgering Frank (pointedly) for being a modernist hipster. The truth is, there is plenty of cross-pollination because we use both modern and classic elements to different degrees in every space we design.

No matter which past one admires, we can't *live* in the past. We are here *now*. As creative people, it is up to us to look forward and make things work for the life people live today. I am obviously in the camp of those who feel that we learn from history by understanding design

precedents. The more I learn about history, the more I realize that little has changed. Humans have always sought out comfort and convenience, and they always will. Certainly the modern age has brought comfort and convenience to more people, which is a very good thing indeed. Owing to new technologies, the cost of many items is generally less expensive than it would otherwise be. Of course, as a classicist, I pine for the days when everything was made entirely by hand, and so I look back longingly to the time before the Industrial Revolution. I'm under no illusion as to what our life would be like without technology, but I can dream, can't I?

But no matter what, the creative spirit stands undaunted. Making things for use and beauty is still an important pursuit that takes enormous effort. It is a process that moves an idea from mind to matter, a procedure filled with potential failure, frustrations, and pitfalls. But in the end, when someone sees the final result and is charmed by it, the endless hours, failed prototypes, and rejection melt away. All that is left is the knowledge that the work was approved and admired.

At White Webb, we design and create mostly interiors, those shockingly short-lived installations for human life. Interestingly enough, we have never designed a house inspired by Italy for a client. Modern Manhattan apartments, Spanish Revival haciendas, rustic mountain cabins, English-inspired houses? Yes. Odd? Not really. We are firm believers that our clients' personalities, not ours, should be reflected in their homes. The rooms in this book are highly personal, reflecting my dreams and passions.

Besides our broad range of interior design projects, we also enjoy creating objects and furnishings. Our Intaglio Collection, with its graphic use of antique engravings, looks both forward and back, using modern technology to craft furnishings of pure fantasy inspired by antiquity.

This collection led to our being invited by Kimberly Davenport to create an installation at the Rice Gallery in Houston, Texas. As designers, it was a huge honor to be invited into the art space—the only one in the United States devoted to installation art.

Later, when we created a collection of acrylic tables, we were inspired by Venetian windows and Islamic architecture—each piece was a modern take on those ancient ideas. These are examples of how we blend my love of Italy and the past with Frank's passion for modern design.

When I was invited to design a collection of silver for the venerable Venetian jeweler Nardi, I completely embraced the past. But no object we've ever designed, whether silver for the table or a table of sparkling acrylic, would exist without the commitment of highly skilled craftspeople—another thing that, even in our modern age, has mercifully remained constant.

There is, however, one object I created that stands apart from those pieces mentioned above. That is the object in your hands at this moment. Like any object of complexity and beauty, this book required the refined skills of a multitude of enormously talented people. I, obviously, could never have created it on my own, and I am forever grateful to those who helped to bring my idea into tangible reality.

It is my sincere hope that *Italy of My Dreams* charms and inspires you. My love of Italy is obvious, but in some ways that's not even the point. If there is one thing I wish for this book to express, it is this: Beauty is not where we find it; it's where we make it.

—Matthew White, December 2009, New York

ABOVE LEFT The cofounders of White Webb, Matthew White, left, and Frank Webb, pose with pieces from their Intaglio Collection, graphic furniture based on antique engravings.

OPPOSITE At the Rice Gallery in Houston, Texas, White Webb created an installation inspired by their Intaglio Collection.

James S. Ackerman, *Palladio*, Penguin, 1966

Marella Agnelli, *Gardens of the Italian Villas*, Rizzoli, 1987

Sofie Bajard and Raffaello Bencini, *Villas and Gardens of Tuscany*, Finest/Éditions Pierre Terrail, 1993

Maria Guila Barberini et al., *Rome Art and Architecture*, Konemann Veslagsgesellschoft, 1999

Fabio Benzi and Caroline Vicenti, *Palaces of Rome*, Rizzoli, 1997

Bruce Boucher, *Andrea Palladio: The Architect in His Time*, Abbeville Press, 1994

Daniela Cinti, *Giardini & giardini: il storico nel centro di Firenze*, Electra, 1997

Peter Coats, *Great Gardens of the Western World*, Spring Books, 1968

Carlo Cresti, *Villas of Tuscany*, The Vendome Press, 1992

Harold Donaldson Eberlein, *Villas of Florence and Tuscany*, Washington Square Press, 1922

Paul and Elizbeth Elek and Moira Johnston, *The Age of the Grand Tour*, Crown, 1967

Marcello Fagiolo, *Roman Gardens: Villas of the City*, Monacelli Press, 2001

Francesco Gurrieri and Patrizia Fabbri, *Palaces of Florence*, Rizzoli, 1995

A. E. Hanson, *An Arcadian Landscape: The California Gardens of A. E. Hansen*, Hennesy & Ingalls, 1985

Henry James, *Italian Hours*, Hoft, 1909

David Garrard Lowe, *Stanford White's New York*, Watson-Guptell, 1999

William L. MacDonald and John A. Pinto, *Hadrian's Villa and Its Legacy*, Yale University Press, 1995

Elisabeth Blair MacDougall, *Fountains, Statues, and Flowers: Studies in Italian Gardens of the Sixteenth and Seventeenth Centuries*, Dumbarton Oaks, 1994

Rosamond E. Mack, *Bazaar to Piazza*, University of California Press, 2002

Georgina Masson, *Italian Villas and Palaces*, Harry N. Abrams, 1959

Giuseppe Mazzriol, *Venetian Palazzi*, Evergreen, 1998

Elizabeth Anne McCauley, *Gondola Days: Isabella Stewart Gardner and the Palazzo Barbaro Circle*, Isabella Stewart Gardner Museum, 2004

The Metropolitan Museum of Art, *Venice and the Islamic World,* Yale University Press, 2007

Agnes Mousnie-Lompre, *Styles italiens*, Plasir de France, 1961

Donatella Mozzoleni, *Palaces of Naples*, Rizzoli, 1999

Michelangelo Muraro and Paolo Marton, *Venetian Villas*, Konemann Verlagsgesellschaft, 1999

Lenore Newman, *A Stanford White Building: The Interior of the Robb House*, S.U.N.Y. Fashion Institute of Technology, 1992

John Julius Norwich, *Paradise of Cities*, Doubleday, 2003

Thorsten Opper, *Hadrian, Empire & Conflict,* The British Museum Press, 2008

Guillermo de Osma, *Fortuny*, Rizzoli, 1980

Giandomenico Romanelli, *Portrait of Venice*, Rizzoli, 1996

John Ruskin, *The Stones of Venice*, Orpington, 1894

James Anthony Ryan, *Frederic Church's Olana*, Black Dome Church, 1989

Witold Rybczynski and Lauren Olin, *Vizcaya*, University of Pennsylvania Press, 2007

Joseph Rykwert, *The Palladian Ideal*, Rizzoli, 1999

Ann Scheid and Robert J. Kelly, *Pasadena: Crown of the Valley*, Windsor Publishing, 1986

Thomas Gordon Smith, *Vitruvius on Architecture*, Monacelli Press, 2003

Robert A. M. Stern, Thomas Mellons, and David Fishman, *New York 1880*, Monacelli Press, 1999

Anthony Thwaite and Peter Porter, *In Italy*, Thames & Hudson, 1974

Gioacchino Lanza Tomasi and Angheli Zalepi, *Palaces of Sicily*, Rizzoli, 1998

Edith Wharton, *Italian Villas and Their Gardens*, The Century Company, 1903

Samuel G. White, *The Houses of McKim, Mead & White*, Rizzoli, 1998

Henry Lionel Williams and Ottalie K. Williams, *Great Houses in America*, G. P. Putnam's Sons, 1969

Alvise Zorzi, *Venetian Palaces*, Rizzoli, 1989

Suggested viewing, a "grand tour" of films, simply for the pleasure of it:

FOR FLORENCE:
A Room with a View (1986)
Director: James Ivory
Producer: Ismail Merchant
Cast: Maggie Smith, Helena Bonham Carter, Julian Sands, Daniel Day Lewis

FOR ROME:
Roman Holiday (1953)
Director: William Wyler
Cast: Gregory Peck, Audrey Hepburn, Eddie Albert

FOR VENICE:
Summertime (1955)
Director: David Lean
Cast: Katharine Hepburn, Rossano Brazzi, Darren McGavin

CREDITS
Unless noted below, all photographs are by Art Gray. Every effort has been made to locate copyright holders; any omission will be corrected in future printings.
Alinari/Art Resource, NY, 70
Courtesy of Amarillo Public Library, 11
Courtesy of the Archives at the Pasadena Museum of History, 110
Photograph by Paulo Ribiero Baptista, 134
Central Synagogue Archives, photo, C.K. Bill, 1872, 106
Photograph by Pat Clark, 14
Courtesy of Collections Artistiques, Galerie Wittert, Université de Liège, 66
Photograph by Dick Davis, 13
Photographs by Stephanie Ellis, idopictures.com, 28
Photographs by John Reed Forsman, forsmanphoto.com, 28, 29, 30, 37, 58, 61, 62, 63, 64, 65
Photograph courtesy of the Friends of Castle Green, 109
Monty Goodson, 16
Photograph by Paul Hester; courtesy of Rice University Art Gallery, 189
C. Don Hughes, 14
Courtesy of Kungl. biblioteket, National Library of Sweden, 18
Courtesy of the Library of Congress, Prints and Photographs Division, LC-USZ62-126974, 134
Courtesy of the Library of Congress, Prints and Photographs Division, LC-USZ62-110672, 132
Courtesy of the Library of Congress, Prints and Photographs Division, HABS NY, 31-NEYO, 120-1, 70
Courtesy of the Library of Congress, Prints and Photographs Division, HABS NY, 11-HUD, 1-2, 107
Image copyright © The Metropolitan Museum of Art/Art Resource, NY, 130
Steven Nilsson, stevennilsson.com, 8, 17, 26, 27, 28, 41, 46, 59, 188
Jeff Oshiro, jeffoshiro.com, 30, 31, 39, 51, 52
Photographs by Aaron Paley, 2, 17
Photograph by Glen Pearson, 16
Erhard Pfeiffer, erhardpfeiffer.com, 31, 32, 45, 54
RIBA Library Photographs Collection, 102
Lee Salem Photography, Inc. salemphoto.com, 29
Scala/Art Resource, NY, 20
Photograph by Thomas Schumacher, 16
Vizcaya Museums & Gardens, Miami, Florida, 22
Dennis Wedlick Architect, 137
Alden White, 10, 11, 13
Photographs by Matthew White, 5, 11, 12, 14, 17, 19, 67, 76, 77, 103, 131, 140, 141, 143, 180, 182, 183, 184, 185, 186, 187
Collection of the author, epi 1-2, 1, 2, 3, 5, 68, 72, 75, 76, 104, 110, 133, 192

Advertising Club (N.Y.C.), 74
Age of Innocence, The (Wharton), 71
Alberti, Leon Battista, 71
Allori, Alessandro, 21
Amarillo (Tex.), 10–12, 13–17
American Academy in Rome, 76
American Renaissance, 71
American Scene, The (James), 7
Ammanati, Bartolomeo, 21
Andalusia, 106
Augustus, bust of, 7, 143

Baldwin, Billy, 12, 31, 143
ballet, 14–15, 16
Baronino, Bartolomeo, 67
Baroque style, 67, 142
Beaux-Arts school, 24
Berenson, Bernard, 21
Berry, Mark, 25
Billy Baldwin Decorates, 12, 31
boxwood, 7, 19, 21, 24, 26, 28

Caesar, Julius, 67
Capitoline Antinous, 142
Casola, Pietro, 103
Castle Green, 7, 108–29
Central Synagogue (N.Y.C.), 106
Chalfin, Paul, 23
Chaucer, Geoffrey, 24
Church, Frederic, 107
Cicero, 188
city houses, 67–101
classical ideals, 67, 71, 73, 76, 105; Palladian style, 131, 133, 135, 138
country villas: Florentine, 19–65; Moorish Revival, 106–7; Palladian, 7, 131–87

Dario, Giovanni, 103, 105, 107
Davenport, Kimberly, 188
Deering, James, 23
Desgodetz, Antoine, 135
Día de los Muertos festival, 13
domes, 7, 108, 131–33, 135
Duquette, Tony, 7, 143

Elliott, Thomas Balch, 110
English country house, 133, 135
Ercole II, Duke of Ferrara, 23

exoticism, 105–7, 108, 110

family crest, 21, 25, 67
Fernbach, Henry, 106
Fitzpatrick, Robert, 16
Florence, 16, 67, 143; villa style, 19–65
Fortuny, 105, 113
Four Books of Architecture (Palladio), 135

garden room, 142
gardens: Amarillo, 10–12; Otium, 143; Roman-style, 19, 21, 23, 24–25, 29, 30; rooftop, 108, 113
geothermal energy, 136, 140
Gibbon, Edward, 67
Gilded Age, 73, 76, 78
Graham, Clare, 113
Grand Canal, 16, 103
grand tour, 13, 78, 113, 135, 143
green systems, 136, 140
Gunston Hall (Va.), 24

Hadrian, Emperor, 131, 133
Hadrian's villa, 140
Harrington mansion (Amarillo), 11, 13
Hayden, Melissa, 15
Hoffman, F. Burrall, 23
Holder, Charles, 110
Hotel Excelsior, 7, 104–5, 108
Hotel Green, 108–10
Hudson River, 107
Hudson Valley, 7, 106–7, 136–40
Hughes Home Beautiful, 13–14
Hunt, Richard Morris, 107
Huntington, Henry E. and Arabella, 24

Intaglio Collection, 188
Islamic style, 103, 105, 106, 107, 188
Italian Renaissance, 67, 71, 73, 76, 131; Venetian style, 105; villas and gardens, 19–23
Italian Revival style, 7, 17; Mediterranean Revival villas, 23–66; nineteenth-century villas, 71–101
Italian Villas and Their Gardens (Wharton), 7, 21
Ixmiquilpan (Mexico), 12–13

James, Henry, 7, 131
Jefferson, Thomas, 135
Jerusalem, 106

Kester, Tom and Maude, 24–25

Lahm, Millicent, 13
Leoni, Giacomo, 135
Lido, 7, 16, 104–5, 108
Lippi, Fra Filippo, 21
Lorenzo the Magnificent, 19, 21
Los Angeles Ballet, 15

Mamluks, 103
Mannerism, 67
Matthew White Antiques and Interiors, 17
Mazzoni, Giulio, 67
McKim, Charles, 73, 76
McKim, Mead, and White, 71, 73
Medici family, 21, 67
Mediterranean Revival style, 23–65
Mehmet II, 105
Metropolitan Museum of Art, 24, 74
Mexico, 12–13
Miami (Fla.), 23
Michelangelo, 71
Mizner, Addison, 23
Molino Viejo, El, 24
Monticello (Va.), 135
Moorish Revival style, 7, 106–29

Nardi, Jacopo, 188
New York City, 69, 71–76, 106
Nureyev, Rudolf, 143
Nutcracker, The (Tchaikovsky), 14–15

Oak Room, 74, 78
Olana, 106–7
Opper, Thorsten, 133
Orientalist art, 105, 106
Otium, 7, 136–87; architecture and site, 136–41; interior design, 142–87
Ottoman Turks, 103, 105

palazzi: nineteenth-century residences, 71–101; Roman, 67–69; Venetian, 103–29
Palazzo Dario, 103
Palazzo de' Rossi, 23

Palazzo Farnese, 67, 71
Palazzo Grimani, 7
Palazzo Spada, 67–70
Palladian country house, 7, 131–35; twenty-first century, 136–87
Palladio, Andrea, 7, 71, 131–33, 135, 138, 140
Pannini, Giovanni Paolo, 78
Pantheon, 16, 131, 133
Pasadena (Calif.), 7, 16–17, 108–10, 113
Patton, George S., Sr., 24
penthouse, 110, 112–13
Pliny the Elder, 19, 21
Pliny the Younger, 19
Poggio, Il, 19–21
Pompey the Great, 67
Porta, Giacomo delle, 71

Raymond Hotel, 107
Renaissance. *See* Italian Renaissance
Rice Gallery (Houston), 188
Robb, Cornelia Van Rensselaer, 7, 73
Robb, James Hampden, 7, 73, 74
Robb House, 7, 69, 73–101
Roehrig, Frederick L., 108
Roman city house, 67–101; nineteenth-century adaptation, 71–101
Roman culture, 19
Romanesque arches, 71
Roman garden, 19, 24–25
Roman palazzo, 67–69
Rome, 16, 76, 131, 143, 188
roof garden, 7, 108, 113
Rose Bowl (Pasadena), 113
roses, 7, 19, 28, 110
Rotunda, La (Villa Capra), 131–33, 135, 142
rotundas, 136, 138, 140
Ruskin, John, 103

Safavids, 103
Salone di Pompeo, 67
San Gabriel Mountains, 108
Sangallo, Antonio da, the Younger, 71
San Marino (Calif.), 17, 24
Sanmicheli, Michele, 7
Sarto, Andrea del, 21
Save Venice, 7, 17
Schneider, Peter, 17
School of American Ballet, 15

Schumacher, Thomas, 15–17, 28
solarium, 108, 110, 112
solar panels, 136, 140
Spada, Bernardino Cardinal, 67
Spada, Virgilio, 67
Spencertown (N.Y.), 136
square tower, 71
Stanfill, Dennis and Terry, 7, 17
Suarez, Diego, 23
synagogues, 106

technology, 188
Texas, 10–12, 143, 188
Tiffany & Co., 7
Tivoli, 140
Tournament of Roses Parade, 110
Tumbleweed Trailer Park, 10, 13
Tuscan villa, 19, 23

Valley Hunt Club, 110
Vaux, Calvert, 107
Venetian carved monkeys, 31, 143
Venetian palace, 103–29
Venice, 7, 16, 17, 103, 131, 143, 188
Victorian pastiche, 71
Vignola, Giacomo da, 71
Villa delle Favole, 7, 17, 24–65, 112, 136, 140
Villa di Poggio a Caiano, 19–21
Villani, Giovanni, 19
Villard Houses, 71–72
villa rustica, 19
villa urbana, 19
Vitruvius, 71
Vizcaya, 23

Webb, Frank, 17, 188
Wedlick, Dennis, 136, 138, 140
Wells, Joseph, 71, 73
Weston, Joe and Eugene, 24, 25
Wharton, Edith, 7, 21, 71
White, Matthew, 7, 10–17, 188
White, Stanford, 7, 69, 71, 73, 74, 76, 78
White Webb, 17, 188
Wilkinson, Hutton, 17

ACKNOWLEDGMENTS

"The ornament of a house is the friends who frequent it."

—Ralph Waldo Emerson

In Sunday school I was taught that everyone is given gifts—God-given talents that must be nurtured and used. But even if one is lucky enough to find those gifts, there is no promise that they will be allowed to shine or even be acknowledged. No matter how great one's gifts are, in order for them to grow, they need love, support, encouragement, and sometimes a good swift kick.

My parents, Kathryn and Alden White, never squashed any dream I ever had, which sadly is something that not every child can say. Of all the blessings a parent can give a child, this to me is the greatest. For that, and for their endless love, I am filled with gratitude.

Of all the people I have ever met, no one has more talents put to better use than my beloved, Thomas Schumacher. He has given the world much more than he has taken, and I have been given more than anyone. His commitment and belief in me surpass description, his love is endless, and his advice (which I sometimes take) is always brilliant. He is my foundation, and this book is for him.

The ability of Alexander de La Kim to create a domestic atmosphere of perfection is simply miraculous. But it is his kindness, love, and endless humor that make our everyday home life a joy.

Without the brilliant vision, great eye, and journalistic gifts of Suzanne Slesin, this book would not have been possible. The fact that she has the most delicious laugh of anyone I know is icing on the cake.

Stafford Cliff is the best book designer of our age. I admired his work long before I ever met him, and I am still counting my blessings that he has spun his magic within these pages.

Art Gray's gifts as a photographer are obvious, but his endless patience and perfectionism put him over the top in my book. The fact that he makes even a control freak like me feel at ease says it all.

Jane Creech of Pointed Leaf Press was a dream to work with. Kind, patient, and professional without ever losing even an ounce of that Southern sweetness I adore. I am also immensely grateful for the work of Jonathan Lazzara, Dominick Santise, and Regan Toews.

John Loring is a good friend and fabulous cook. The fact that he has a near-encyclopedic knowledge of art, design, and architecture is just part of the brilliant package. I am fortunate that he has been in my corner for many years and that he penned his eloquent words the first time I appeared in *Architectural Digest*.

I have been blessed with mentors who have impacted my life more than they can know.

Terry Stanfill, a lady of great style, with a deep love for Italy, first introduced me to Save Venice. She is my dear friend, and one day I hope to have a garden half as beautiful as hers. Edwin Monsson and Tony Greco at one time had the most perfect antiques shop in Los Angeles, called Edwin-Anthony. I have learned through their example what taste can be, and I adore them both.

My business partner, Frank Webb, puts up with a lot. In spite of my eye-rolling, I really do like the "classic versus modern" debate, and sometimes I even learn something.

I am forever in debt to the following friends and colleagues. Each one has encouraged, mentored, provided inspiration, and supported me in innumerable ways: Alba and Marco Alvarado, Jaye Anderton, Alan Barlis, Mark Berry, Contessa Simonetta Brandolini d'Adda, Debbie and John Brincko, Paul Burgess, Karen McElroy Carroll, Mary Lea and Bill Carroll, Lisa Chai, Pat Clark, Melissa Conn, Paolo Costagli, Kimberly Davenport, Mary Donnelly-Crocker, Annie and John Fiorilla, Maureen Footer, Wendy Goodman, Bob Breen and Clare Graham, Carol Gretter, Beatrice and Randolph H. Guthrie, Adria de Haume, Christine and Scott Hayward, Gregg Herbert, Camille and Neil Hess, the Hughes family, Candace and Michael Humphreys, Hillary Hunter, Doug Huntington, Frederick Ilchman, Aubrey James, Tanya Jonsson, Scott Jordan, Georgie Kajer, Mary Lou Kerston, Tom Kester, Mary Kay Konfal, Jason Kontos, David Krueger, Peter Iocano and Manfred Kuhnert, Katherine Kuster, Janice Langrell, Michael Lassell, Carmen Leon, Natrelle Long, Gene Maiden, Elizabeth Makrauer, Jim Marrin, Karen Marshall, Jason Money, Peter Mulderry, Alberto Nardi, Samantha Nestor, Lenore Newman, Jennifer Chueng and Steven Nilsson, Elinor Nordskog, Linda O'Keefe, Moose Moravec and Anne Osberg, Violet Ouyang, Mitchell Owens, Dale Pearson, Dean Pearson, Glen Pearson, Tony and Keith Perrino, Francesca Bortolotto Posatti, Dagna Recewicz, Paige Rense, Suzanne Rheinstein, Marion Riley-Campbell, Nicolo Rubelli , Margaret Russell, Elsie Sadler, Frank Scheuer, Steve Schroko, Peg Schumacher, Giampaolo Seguso, Gianluca Seguso, Pierpaolo Seguso, Dan Shaw, Sarah Shelton, Matt Sinclair, Sonya Sinha, Cecilia Soto, Dennis Stanfill, Cathy Grier and Michele Steckler, Rica Tarnoff, Barbara Thornburg, Jorge Vargas, Kris Vickery, Dennis Wedlick, Joe and Joy Weston, Ruth and Hutton Wilkinson, Terry Wolverton, Cathy and Robert Woolway, Sarah Zorn, and the entire board of Save Venice Inc. —M.W.

FRONT ENDPAPERS LEFT AND BACK ENDPAPERS An eighteenth-century reinterpretation of a typical eighth-or-ninth-century motif that includes flora and fauna both real and imagined. These designs have roots in Persia but became very popular in Italy.

FRONT ENDPAPERS RIGHT Saplings from the surrounding forest adorn the living room of Otium, Matthew White's house in the Hudson Valley. The room, furnished with Italian antiques, has an eighteenth-century painting resting on the limestone mantel.

FRONT ENDPAPERS VERSO The detail from a plaster ceiling panel is from the Robb House, in New York City, by architect Stanford White.

HALF TITLE This eighteenth-century Italian engraving depicts a branch tied to a fluted column with a silk sash—perhaps representing the marriage of natural and man-made worlds.

OPPOSITE CONTENTS At dusk, the Tuscany-inspired guesthouse at the Villa delle Favole is reflected in the formal swimming pool.

BACK COVER This early-nineteenth-century, neo-classic bust of a young man sports a necklace by Tony Duquette, one of America's most unique designers.

Pointed Leaf Press, LLC.
136 Baxter Street,
New York, NY 10013
www.pointedleafpress.com

Printed and bound in China.

First edition
10 9 8 7 6 5 4 3 2 1
Library of Congress Control Number: 2009940676
ISBN 13: 978-0-9823585-2-8